A711/84

C000137237

A ROUND WITH DARWIN

A ROUND WITH DARWIN

A Collection of the Golf Writings

of

Bernard Darwin

SOUVENIR PRESS

Edited and compiled by MARGARET HUGHES

Copyright © Mrs Ursula Mommens, Lady Darwin
and the Estate of Mrs N. Fenn
Compilation and introduction © Souvenir Press Ltd.,
and Margaret Hughes 1984

First published 1984 by Souvenir Press Ltd,
43 Great Russell Street, London WC1B 3PA
and simultaneously in Canada

All Rights Reserved. No part of this publication
may be reproduced, stored in a retrieval system,
or transmitted, in any form or by any means, electronic,
mechanical, photocopying, recording or otherwise without
the prior permission of the Copyright owner

ISBN 0 285 62664 7

Photoset in Great Britain by
Rowland Phototypesetting Ltd,
Bury St Edmunds, Suffolk
Printed in Great Britain by
Biddles of Guildford

EDITOR'S NOTE

The great pianist Arthur Schnabel used often to say that, although he had no knowledge of cricket and had never been to a match, he nevertheless knew what went on during a day's play by reading the writing of Neville Cardus.

The same could be said about the golf writing of Bernard Darwin. For many years he attracted not only the golfing public but also a host of non-players who had no idea of the difference between a niblick and a mashie.

I have chosen the essays in this book because I think they epitomise the excellence and charm of his writings on golf; I hope that they will give readers as much pleasure as they have given me over the years.

CONTENTS

GOOD RESOLUTIONS

The coming of each New Year's Day brings with it for golfers, as for other people, reflections on the past and resolutions for the future. As to the resolutions, we often have a greater opportunity of making them than of putting them into practice, for in the early days of January there is apt to be a wind so biting, even if the links be not carpeted with snow, that the wise man lays aside his clubs and the foolish one confines his attention to a captive ball. Reflections are always open to us, but, as we grow older, they are apt to become just a little sad. One of the more depressing that gradually forces itself upon us is that that which we are pleased to term "our game" is never going to get any better. There was a time when we hoped that a miracle would occur, and that the dash and strength and glory of hitting which are vouchsafed to the few might suddenly one fine morning descend upon us too, so that we should be as creatures transfigured and made splendid for evermore. Braid says that he went to bed a short driver and woke up a long one, and we, without knowing that curious piece of natural history, yet trusted that something of the kind was going to happen to us.

After a certain number of Januaries we know in our heart of hearts that that beautiful New Year's day-dream is not coming true. We may possibly be going to play very well in the coming year: better and more steadily, perhaps, than we have ever played before; but it will be our own old second-rate game, with just one or two mistakes the less, or perhaps a long-continued putting inspiration. We shall not really be hitting the ball any better, but just because we are not eating or drinking or smoking too much, or because we have got a new club that gives us confidence, we may be making fewer bad shots. Heaven knows that this is not a state of things to be despised, for it will lead to the acquisition of many half-crowns, but there is a pang in realising that we never shall tear the ball away with the brassy from a deep cup and send it hurtling on to a green two hundred yards away: never play those wonderful low, forcing shots with the iron that burrow their way through a solid wall of wind. We shall never do these heroic things, because we simply have not got it in us. And so we have just got to make the best of our own permanently pedestrian attainments.

Well, it is depressing, but the fact that we recognise our own limitations, or so at least we flatter ourselves, argues that there is in us a measure of sense and knowledge of the game which a good many people lack. I believe that there are golfers who think—nay, I have heard them say it—that the only difference between their game and that of Braid is that he does the holes in four more often than they do. They do not see any material distinction, between the hole as played by them and by a champion. They take two full shots, neither hit perfectly clean, a long putt from the outskirts of the green laid within five feet, and the fourth scrambled in: he has a drive, a crisp, firm half-shot with an iron, and a six-yard putt that goes in and out of the hole for three. Both holes were done in four, but that is the only point of resemblance. Yet there are some who, because they can sometimes successfully bring off these two half-hit drives and that scrambling putt throughout a whole round, imagine in their secret souls that they have for once attained to the level of really first-class golf. Let us pray to be delivered from similar blindness, even though it is wonderfully pleasant for a time.

If it is saddening to know that we have arrived, roughly speaking, at our fixed place in golfing society, increasing age can offer some compensating consolations. The small boy who is suddenly deprived of some eagerly expected pleasure cannot believe in the possibility of any further happiness in this world. He may not eat that bun or go to that children's party; therefore it is absurd—nay, it is actually insulting—to suggest that there can ever be other buns and other parties or any pleasure to be derived from them. In the same way, the young golfer who is in the throes of a hideous golfing malady cannot believe that the ball which now flies in a malignant curve to the right will one day go straight down the course again. It must surely be, he thinks, that he is condemned to slice for ever; he utterly refuses to admit the possibility of any improvement, even though he is trying a new swing every minute in order to effect one. After a certain number of years he learns by experience that no golfing disease—not even slicing—does go on for ever, and that the day will come when he will hit the ball again. Of course, he learns also that he will miss it again, that there is nothing before him but a series of hits and misses to the end of the chapter, whereas the callow youth, having once got rid of his slice, cannot believe that it will ever recur, and strikes the stars with his uplifted head accordingly. Which is better? Alternating despair and rapture, or an equable cynicism?

I said that New Year's Day reflections were gloomy, but I had no idea how gloomy they would be till I came to write them down. Now that I see them in black and white, I grow ashamed of a spirit so whimpering and unmanly. After all, I force myself to say, things are not really so very bad, and Mr. Charles Hutchings won the championship when he was fifty-three, and I am going to the course I love best in the world, and the weather looks promising. I shall play with some who are quite old and fat, and I can give them strokes—quite a lot of strokes. I must go and pack up my clubs—I am sure I shall improve this year, after all.

That, beyond doubt, is the braver spirit, and so, with all the old buoyant hopefulness, let us leave reflection and fall to upon our good resolutions for yet another year. What are they to be? They must be of a noble and lofty character, dealing with the general principles of golfing wisdom, and not stooping to some small trick or mannerism that we have discovered, and which, we fondly believe, has cured us permanently of some fell disease. These things are but evanescent: though at the moment we believe them to be among the eternal verities. We know that we make twenty or thirty such discoveries every year. Our New Year's resolutions must be on broader lines.

The first one that would rise to most golfers' minds is probably the best and most far-reaching—"Be up." Be up in our putts, be up in our short approaches, be up with any shot whereby we try to reach the green. How many strokes and half-crowns we should save, how very few holes we should lose, by being past the hole! The hole will not come to us, and yet to reach it is the hardest thing in the whole world of golf. There must surely be some scientific explanation of this almost universal failing. If our long approach, a little too firmly played, run over the green into a bunker, we are commiserated on all sides; nobody says "Bad luck!" if the shot drop feebly into trouble short of the green. Therefore the former disaster should clearly be less annoying than the latter. Why, then, do we not court it more strenuously? It is more common to be short, because it is so much more common to underclub rather than to overclub ourselves. Most people are more at ease with a spoon than a brassy, a driving iron than a spoon, and so on down to the mashie. They feel happier with the shorter club, and take it for safety if they have any excuse for doing so. Consequently they are often short from taking a club with which under no circumstances could they be up to the flag; if they do not hit the ball quite clean, they are, of course, shorter still.

One reason for this underclubbing is that for the average golfer it is less disastrous to press at a shot than to spare one. This is a bold statement, and is opposed to the views of those eminent persons who declare that it is easier to play a half-shot with a powerful club than a full shot with a less powerful one. I do not believe that for the average golfer this last doctrine is true. He finds himself, let us say, 150 or 160 yards from the hole. Should he take his cleek he will be worried with the feeling that he is going too far; result, he will spare it, tuck his arms into his body instead of following through properly, and hook or slice the ball a thousand miles away. If he take his iron he may hit rather too hard, and make an indifferent shot, but the disaster will not be of the same magnitude. He will thus gradually get into a habit of taking the shorter club, and, as a result, his approaches will very generally be short of the hole.

A very good golfer once told me that he attributed a great part of his success to the fact that when in doubt between two clubs he always took the stronger one. On the other hand, another fine player, especially good with his cleek, informed me that he often took his cleek, even though he knew he could not quite get up with it, in preference to a brassy. Of these two teachers the second was the greater player, but his precepts appear the less sound: his tenets should be regarded as part of the eccentricity of his genius, and not to be imitated.

Another good resolution to make, at least from a match-winning point of view, would be that during a match one should concentrate one's entire attention on hitting the ball, and reserve all heart-searchings as to the causes of wrong-doing till the time of practice after the round. If we once begin to wonder in the middle of a game what we are doing wrong in executing some particular stroke, we lose interest in all other strokes, so that our whole game becomes disjointed, and any temporary improvement in respect of the diseased stroke is outweighed by a general feebleness and uncertainty in other departments. Probably every golfer has some word of wisdom, appropriate to himself, that he can add to this little New Year's sermon. We can always fall back on those precepts which are part of general as well as golfing morality, such as not to call one's opponent's best shot a beastly fluke or to pursue an irritating caddy with a niblick. These, however, are matters rather for the spiritual than the golfing pastor.

Of a different kind to these wise resolves made before a roaring fire, or haply as we lie snugly in bed listening to the wintry wind, are those that we make at the beginning of a summer holiday. There can surely be few more agreeable sensations in life than that of settling comfortably down for some considerable time in the neighbourhood of a first-class seaside golf course. We have ecstatic visions of all we are going to do: the final polish to be put upon the cruder of our armoury of shots, the deadly solidity of steadiness to which we shall attain. There need be none of that feverish anxiety to be up and at it which attends a brief visit of a few days. No, we will go about the business temperately and soberly. We will attend to our other avocations in the morning, loaf down after lunch, and practise some of those shots, and perhaps play one round in the cool of the evening. What-ever we do we will not play ourselves into a state of dotage by means of three rounds a day; practice is the way to improve and to practice we will devote a great part of our energies.

It is said that the great Mr. Travis, when he was educating himself to win our championship and that of his own country, would go out with a dozen balls and work away at just one shot for an hour and a half at a stretch. A gentleman who has been staying at our seaside course is working away on the same lines, and has brought his handicap down from 18 to 3 in less than no time. What a bright example! We will map out an elaborate educational schedule, and stick to it through thick and thin. First of all, of course, there is the art of driving, which is said to be the easiest thing in the world, when one is in constant practice, and which, beyond all doubt, is abominably difficult when one is not. We have often driven well for short spells, and have been hazily conscious of a series of sensations which have accompanied our success. Now we will run those sensations to earth, if such a metaphor be permissible, discover exactly what is the cause of them, and what exactly we are doing, and then, of course, it will be quite easy to drive well and steadily ever afterwards.

Now here in the very beginning the system will probably break down, and what will really happen will be something entirely different. After a few days, if it be not presumptuous to hope so much, we shall very likely begin to drive quite respectably, just because we have had those few consecutive days' golf, and the club feels a familiar and comfortable thing. We shall, as we imagine, solve the mystery and attribute our success to some particular action which may have temporarily something to do with it. In all our preliminary swings we shall be careful to introduce and indeed exaggerate that action; and yet, in spite of our folly, we may not improbably continue to drive well, just because we are in good practice, and can therefore afford to do some foolish things and yet hit the ball. So at the end of our summer-time we set out for home under the blissful delusion that we have mastered driving once and for all. Alas! we shall soon find, when we return to week-end habits again, that the virtue lay not in that particular kink or switch; that, had we only known it, had long since become a piece of useless lumber, and the secret was merely that of frequent play. Hope, of course, springs

more or less eternal in every golfer's breast, or the suicide
statistics would long since have been such as to arouse the
attention of all thoughtful citizens. It was not very long since
that I saw a gentleman but moderately old and extremely
eminent in other walks of life, putting in an attitude of
unconscionable discomfort, his right foot tucked far away
behind his left, so that he leered at the ball over his left
shoulder. This position, he declared, enabled him to keep
his eye on the ball. I wonder how long it was before that
ever-youthful spirit returned, chastened and humble, to his
natural attitude, in which, by the way, he putts more than
reasonably well.

I find, despite all my show of bravery for the New Year,
that I grow cynical and depressed again over the memories of
many summer holidays, and, among the disappointments
that I recall, there are scarce any more poignant than those
connected with the new club that I bought before setting out.

Why is it that a man becomes temporarily demented as
soon as he enters a shop with the intention of buying a club?
I do not allude to the fact that he spends his money on
Dreadnoughts, when he ought to be getting bread for his
starving children. He may be perfectly justified in buying a
club, but he goes perfectly mad in choosing *the* club that he
does buy. The moment he crosses the threshold and sees the
tempting array of clubs, with their nice shining heads and
their handles sacrificially adorned with pink paper, he loses
all idea of the kind of club he wants. Put him on a golf course,
and he would instantly reject the proffered implement. "As
flat as a skate," he would say; or would dismiss it with
justifiable contempt as more suitable for a cricket bat. In the
shop, however, he becomes incapable of judging of the lie of
a club; and he will buy one absurdly flat, or upright, as the
case may be, and bear it home in unsuspecting triumph, only
to find out on his first visit to the links that he has irretrievably
wasted seven and sixpence.

Nor is it only as regards the lie that we lose our wits; our
"judgment goes out a-wisitin'" equally in the matter of
weight. A little while ago, a most excellent golfer showed me
with some pride a new brassy. It was an admirable club, but
had only become so through having had very nearly all the

lead taken out, so that there was a perfect chasm in the back of the head. Yet its owner, one of the sanest of mankind in the ordinary way, had bought it in a shop under the impression that it exactly suited him in its primitive state.

I may perhaps quote myself as another and more aggravated instance of this lunacy. Some time ago I bought a kind of medium iron or "jigger." I bought it because I thought that it was a little more upright in the lie than the one I already possessed, and also, I must confess, because it had a crooked neck, which exercised a weird fascination over me. The moment I took it out on to the grass the scales dropped from my eyes, and I saw the club as it really was. It is, in fact, considerably flatter than my old friend; its neck is in the last degree distasteful to me, and it has a shaft so abominably supple that it twists out of my hand like an eel. Some day, when I have had a new shaft put in, and have caused the head to be bent in a fiery furnace, it may possibly be a passable club, but it will have been a very expensive one.

The vendors of clubs do wisely when they pitch their tents not upon the edge of the links, but in the heart of a great city. The additional rent that they have to pay must be a drop in the ocean compared with the sums that we pay them for clubs we shall never be able to play with. Whether it is that we cannot judge of a club when we are arrayed in tall hats and tail coats, or whether there is something subtly deceitful about a hard level floor in place of yielding and uneven turf, I do not know; but, as a rule, the only possible verdict on our actions is one of temporary insanity.

When we are once more in our right mind we have to decide on what to do with the new purchase, since we cannot play with it. Obviously, our first attempt should be to sell it to a friend at as slight a reduction as possible. It may really be that what is our poison will be his meat, in which case we can proceed in an honest and straightforward manner. If that is not possible, we must, of course, take care that he should not have any opportunity of trying the club on a golf course, since he will at once detect its faults. We must lure him into our own house. The surroundings of an ordinary house are not so seductive as those of a shop, but still there is a reasonable hope that he will be deceived.

If we cannot sell the club, we must either throw it away or put it away, and the latter is the preferable course. For one thing, clubs are very difficult things to throw away. I once tried to throw away some old clubs by putting them in the waste-paper basket together with socks that were all holes and collars frayed past redemption. The socks and collars disappeared, but a too-faithful servant carefully replaced the clubs in the corner whence they had been extracted. Then, too, clubs, like razors, sometimes become reformed characters through a period of enforced seclusion. Put them in a cupboard till they are coated with rust and dirt. Nine will remain useless, but the tenth will emerge, having been born again in some mysterious way, the club we have been dreaming of.

It should be added that it is only when we are buying clubs for ourselves that we act so insanely. If our intention is to purchase a *gage d'amour* for a golfing friend, we may have the utmost confidence in our judgment. We shall inevitably pick out a club the most perfectly balanced in the world. The shaft will be a miracle of "steeliness," having the "music," to use Tom Morris's word, exactly in the right place, and the lines of the head will be such as bring tears to the eye. I have at different times bought several clubs for a near relation. Two of them have now found their way back to my own bag, and it is only an innate chivalry that restrains me from stealing a third. As to the two she has really no solid ground of complaint, for they were obviously too heavy for her, and I handed over in exchange an admirable specimen of the Schenectady putter. As I have pointed out to her with excellent clear common sense, I could not be expected to know that the Rules of Golf Committee were going to bar it.

SOME UNREPORTED HISTORY

There are few who can, like the principal characters in Mr. Wilkie Collins's novels, fly to their diaries at the end of each day, and deliver themselves of a narrative, full of stirring incident and varying emotion, to the extent of several closely printed pages. To write accounts on this scale of all their rounds of golf would be too much for the most enthusiastic and egotistical of golfers; to keep a golfing diary, however, of a more modest kind is rather an amusing occupation. Such a diary is usually little more than a bare record of facts, a business-like production, suggestive of book-keeping by double entry, with different columns for the venue of the match, name of opponent, result, general remarks, and the player's score, if his play has been accurate enough, or his perseverance great enough to enable him to keep one.

The golfer should aim at absolute honesty in his diary, if he does not want his conscience to torture him in after years. He must write the truth, and nothing but the truth, though lack of space will prevent him putting down the whole truth about each round. The achievement is not really so difficult as it might appear. To play a round alone—in itself an impossible occupation—and keep a perfectly accurate score is a test of truthfulness too high for the most scrupulous, for the short putts will count themselves as holed, when, in fact, the ball hung on the lip.

A match, however, is a different thing; the result is clear-cut and definite and cannot be misstated; sometimes, indeed, there is positively a savage satisfaction in inscribing: "Lost by seven and six; played abominably." After a bad disaster there is really no temptation to palter with one's honesty; the naked truth and a "nice derangement of epitaphs" in the remarks column gives the greatest relief to the feelings.

I have called a golfing diary a bare record of facts, but the baldest statement can recall a flood of memories. The entry: "November, Mudley-in-the-Hole. Lost to Jones by one hole," brings back the whole horrid scene to the mind. In a flash the drear darkness of the November day is around us, and we feel the rich clay soil of the Mudley course squelching about our boots: then we recall the dreadful fact that we have tried to banish from the mind that we were three up and four to play, and actually lost the match. The holes began to drop off "like snow off a dyke," and we cracked; that detestable Jones, who had previously been extremely depressed and ill-humoured, became endowed with a new confidence and a joviality far more trying than any depression—and we let him win all those last four holes! That is the worst of a golfing diary: it reminds us of things that we must forget if we are to go out in a proper spirit to do battle. Perhaps the best thing to do is to turn to a later entry: "September, St. Andrews. Beat Jones by two and one after being three down at the turn." That is indeed a glorious recollection; we remember how "dourly" we stuck to our adversary and wore him down, so that his mood underwent a variation, the exact converse of the one before described. And yet the recalling of old triumphs does not instil confidence half so surely as the remembrance of ignominy destroys it. After all, perhaps this is rather hysterical, and the golfer has no business to be such a creature of emotions. The bitterness of disaster should soon lose its sting, while there is a permanent satisfaction in a page where the score column is dotted with totals beginning with seven, and sometimes with the details of a bright, particular round set out *in extenso*, those pretty little rows, fours and threes and occasional fives—I am letting my imagination run riot—which bespeak a red-letter day.

If any one be encouraged to begin a golfing diary, let him beware of obtruding it too freely on the notice of his fellow-golfers. If he does not follow this advice, he will probably find the effect on unwilling readers akin to that produced on Mr. Pickwick by Mr. Pott's leading articles in the *Eatanswill Gazette*, when we are told that "his eyes were closed as if with excess of pleasure during the whole time of their perusal." It is a curious but well-ascertained fact that the narration of our own golf matches, like that of our own remarkable dreams, is likely to be of infinitely greater interest to ourselves than to others. Our listeners are inevitably bored, and, if they remain affable, it is only because they hope ultimately to secure us as audience for a longer and duller history.

Some there are, even among the ranks of good players, men cast in an heroic mould, who really prefer to watch a good match to playing themselves, and whose conversation deals with the feats of others rather than their own. Consideration is of course due to the poor week-end golfer, who crams all his play into a day and a half, and whose interest, therefore, must almost inevitably be concentrated on his own game. It is therefore fair to add that the Olympian creatures before described are usually persons of ample leisure, who have plenty of time in which to play themselves, besides that which they devote to studying the golf of others.

Let the diary-keeper, then, be not too prodigal of treasures from his store. There are, of course, pig-headed persons who will not be convinced that their recollection of golfing incidents is not as clear as our own; for the purpose of refuting these the diary will be invaluable, and may legitimately be produced. Otherwise the wise man will read over his diary only in private, when he wishes to revive pleasing and tender memories of the good times he has enjoyed upon the links.

As a rule, the keeper of a diary has enough to do in recording his own matches, and has little room for those of other people. I profess myself no exception to this rule of selfishness. And yet, as I turn the pages, I come across one or two records that strike me as entertaining, even though I played but a wholly passive part in the performance. There is, for one, the singular affair of the cross-country journey at Rye.

One has often heard stories of these cross-country golfing feats and very seldom seen them. There is, for instance, a legend that an intrepid gentleman undertook to play from Maidstone to Littlestone, a distance of something over thirty miles. The feat involved the playing of several shots through the public streets, a possible difference of opinion with the local authorities, and, so history records, a loss of thirty-seven balls. How many thousand strokes he was allowed I do not know, but he won his bet. Let us hope it was a substantial one to compensate him for the loss of his thirty-seven florins.

Personally I had never witnessed any such achievement till on this occasion at Rye, and then it was on quite a modest scale. We had a high wind that day upon the course, which, it may be added, is a demoniacally windy spot. It blew so hard about luncheon time that A. betted B. that he would not play from the sixth tee to the eleventh hole in five-and-twenty shots. As events turned out, this would have been a most judicious move on the part of the crafty A., if the wind had continued to blow from the same quarter with the same violence. As it was, fortune favoured the brave, and about 4.30 the wind began to veer round, till finally from being dead in B.'s teeth, it blew nearly straight across his course. Moreover, it blew from left to right, and B., like most frail mortals, preferred a hook to a slice. For those who know the Rye course no explanation is necessary; for those who have that pleasure to come it may be said that B.'s course lay more or less straight from tee to hole with a slight bend to the left for the last lap.

By the terms of the wager he had till six o'clock, and started out about five full of hope and tea, attended by a small gallery. We felt a distinct thrill as, at about 5.15, he solemnly teed his ball for its long journey. The sensation was in a small way something like that which, I should imagine, would be experienced in waiting for an aeroplane to start; not unlike the voyages of some aeroplanes, the journey itself proved in the end a little disappointing. However, the initial thrill was indisputable; "He's off," we whispered, and the first shot landed safely out of harm's way. Almost immediately came one of the crucial moments of the journey. About the distance of two full shots from the tee is a row of coastguards' cottages surrounded by small gardens, while the situation was complicated by a Bank Holiday tea party indulging in a tug-of-war near the sixth green. B., however, gave them a wide berth, slogging doggedly along with a rather stumpy, battered-looking short spoon, and at about 5.20 a bulletin might have been issued: "Coastguards safely passed; going strong."

After this came a good long spell of open country, and B.

made excellent progress with his spoon. Occasionally he went perilously near trouble, but to the obvious disappointment of the gallery he would not get into it. If he went in the direction of a bunker he always lay just short of it, while if the ball disappeared into long grass ("up to his neck," as we said hopefully) it was always found lying comfortably upon a narrow footpath; A. grew gradually grey with passion, and murmured something about "infernal luck." The only hope of disaster now lay in a narrow neck which comes after the ninth green. There is a public-house on the right, a hard high road in the middle, and a row of sandhills on the left. Over the sandhills there is grass, and there is also a narrow strip of turf on this side, between the road and the sandhills, but with any luck the gallery opined he must get into something.

Now, if B. had not shown us what he meant to do, we should have thought his next shot a great one. Unfortunately, by humanely moving two small children from the strip of turf, he clearly indicated that he intended to lie between the road and the sandhills, whereas as a matter of fact, a fine hooky spoon shot, with the wind at its tail, carried road, strip, sandhills, and all, and deposited the ball safely on the far side. A. was furious, while B. declined to say more than that he had tried to hit the ball. After this all was plain sailing, with the exception of one bad lie—he ought to have had several—and he was left with the prospect of a score of twenty easily within his grasp. Fired with the ambition to do nineteen, however, B. essayed a breakneck carry over a cabbage garden, and went out of bounds. This sobered him a little. He finally holed out with extreme caution in twenty-two strokes, having only played two shots, save on the green, with anything but a wooden club—a testimony alike to his good spoon and his good fortune.

There was not a scene of great enthusiasm at the finish, nor did anybody frantically embrace B. The only thing that ensued was an acrimonious discussion as to whether he would have done it if the wind had continued to blow, he declaring that he would just have managed it, we, one and all, asserting that he would never have got past the public-house.

Leaving Rye and turning over a few more pages I come to another pleasant course in Sussex, Ashdown Forest, and another, as I hope, pleasant little bit of golfing history that has never been reported. As to reports of golf matches in general, it will, I suppose, be conceded that they make excessively dull reading. This is not wholly the fault of the reporters; it arises from the fact that there is nearly always a lamentable lack of incident. So blameless is the play that the reporters are sometimes driven to fabricate exciting events. Thus we may read that Braid "pulled his drive and sliced his second going to the third hole." Yet when we study the score we observe that for this, as it appears, scandalously played hole, the champion obtained an orthodox four. The real fact of the matter, of course, was that whereas at all the other holes both his shots were perfectly straight, at this one hole he did hit slightly to the left of the guide flag off the tee, while his approach landed the ball at least a dozen yards to the right of the hole.

How far more entertaining it would be if the professionals were left severely alone and the Press recorded a few of the so-called ordinary games (they are really of absorbing interest) which take place daily on any course. There would be no need for manufactured incident. On the contrary, there would be ample opportunity for exercising that masterly reticence which distinguishes the greatest works of literature. A few of the leading features would fill a column; fully spun out, an eighteen-hole match would run to a three-volume novel. It is really to prove this point that I venture to give the briefest possible narrative of just one hole that I once saw played by two friends of mine. There is not a word in it that is not absolutely true.

The two players I will call W. and G. They both have handicaps well advanced in double figures, and the chief difference between them is that W. plays right-handed and G. is under the impression that he does better with left-handed clubs. The hole in question was the second hole at Ashdown Forest. It is an excellent hole: in length, I suppose, some 360 or 380 yards, and bristling with difficulties. In front of the tee the ground rises steadily to the crest of a hill some 120 yards away, and is full of cavernous ruts. On the top of the hill is a patch of turf: then comes a belt of thick heather: then another patch of turf, and, finally, the green admirably guarded by various ditches. With these preliminary observations, I may embark on Chapter I. of the narrative, and unless the reader indulges in the meanness of "looking on" to the end, he will have no idea who is going to win the hole till the last of the "hair-breadth 'scapes" is over.

W. had the honour, and hit a shot that would have been a very good one at the first hole at St. Andrews—I will call it a "low, raking drive." The ball hit the face of the hill some little way below the crest and sat down in a rut. G. now teed his ball, and after a somewhat ornate waggle, missed it by several inches. He remarked that he had not done that for some time, and advanced once more to the assault. This time there was, to quote from the Rules of Golf, a "contact between the head of the club and the ball resulting in movement of the ball"; it moved a perceptible distance, but remained on the teeing ground. At the third attempt he got going in earnest, and sent the ball some way up the hillside, where it might have remained on a little refuge of turf if it had not elected to fall into a narrow drain. G. lifted under a penalty of one stroke, and played the four more—a masterly iron shot which deposited the ball in temporary safety on the first patch of fairway.

We must now leave G. for a while, and return to W. His first niblick shot moved the ball from one rut to repose its scarred and furrowed countenance in another; his second put it into some heather to the right; his third shot with an iron (being his fourth shot all told) sent it flying well over the heather, to lie not far from the ditch guarding the green, so that he might reasonably entertain hopes of a seven. G. now played the two more—his sixth shot—and also reached a satisfactory strategic base from which to pitch over the ditch. His seventh saw him safely on the green about five yards from the hole.

Now came the crucial one off two as played by W. The ball was appreciably lofted, so much I must admit; but it was far too short and was obviously about to bury itself in the ditch. In a moment the whole aspect of the game had changed; W. would infallibly have to lift under penalty preparatory to playing the like from behind the water hazard, and poor despised G., who stands on the wrong side of his ball, would be certain of a half at the very least. Now we reach the turning-point of the hole, and perhaps, indeed, of the match. W.'s ball pitched fairly and squarely into the ditch, but by some miraculous means bounced out again and lay on the green. He took the regulation three putts to hole out, and won the hole in a superbly played eight. The sympathies of the spectator could not be otherwise than warmly engaged on G.'s behalf. He played a terribly uphill game with magnificent coolness and daring, and I vow that it was only bad luck that prevented him from winning the hole. W., as his once overwhelming advantage dwindled, was growing perceptibly nervous, and if he had once got into that ditch it is my firm conviction that he would never have got over it. What is more, W. ultimately won the match by a single putt on the last green, so that on that one outrageous piece of good luck hung the whole fortunes of the day.

Possibly I am prejudiced, but the account of that one hole appears to me more interesting than that of a whole round played by the whole Triumvirate. If it is not, then it is owing to the imperfections of the narrative rather than to an inherent weakness in the incidents, for I never saw half such an entertaining hole in my life. Oh, why was there no cinematograph there to record its varied episodes for all eternity?

When I am a millionaire I propose to have my own private cinematograph which shall record all the more pleasing incidents of my golfing career. The bad shots, the gnashing of teeth, and the hurling of clubs—these I shall bury in decent oblivion, but as to the few, very few really good shots, of these I shall never tire. There was a certain stymie that I once successfully lofted at the nineteenth hole. If I only had that recorded—my own glee, my adversary's face of gloom, my ball just disappearing into the hole—how I would "lean and love it over again." Meanwhile my progress on the road towards Park Lane is so far inconsiderable, and the only occasion in which I have seen golf on a biograph was at a music-hall, when it proved well worth waiting for, even through the intolerable tedium of a ballet.

To one wholly ignorant of the why or wherefore of anything even remotely mechanical, the pace at which things happen on the biograph must always be mysterious. One has seen the crews at the May Races at Cambridge rowing—bio-graphically—a stroke with which no crew on this side of the Styx could hope to compete. On visiting the music-hall, therefore, one is prepared to see the professionals refuting that respectable old maxim "slow back" even more emphatically than they naturally do. This is not so, however: the swing seems to perform itself at its normal pace—indeed, one is rather struck by the slowness of it—but the moment the ball is hit, crowd and players appear to rush after the ball at a pace suggestive rather of a record time than a record score.

The putting is the really exciting part of the affair. To see a ball disappear into a hole is always either deightful or horrible, according to whether we ourselves or our opponents have struck it, but in either case there is a moment in which to prepare ourselves when we see the ball making straight for the hole.

On the biograph, however, we hardly see the hole: there is only a ball slithering over a grey carpet and suddenly disappearing. It is really rather thrilling, especially as we are in the position never attained by human golfer of knowing the future. Coming events cast their shadows before in the form of an announcement on the screen, "A. Herd holes an Eleven-yard Putt." We see Herd strike his ball and encourage it with wild gesticulations of his club. He is evidently under the impression that he has not given it enough "legs," but we know better, and, sure enough, a crevice suddenly opens in the ground and the ball vanishes.

Then a gentleman appears on the screen, about to attack a ridiculously short putt. We wonder why we are not told who he is, till we see his lamentable effort, when we understand that out of charity the management has suppressed his name. Before he can show signs of disgust at his failure he and his spectators flit rapidly away, to make room for the announcement, "T. Drummond misses a Two-foot Putt." Now, here would appear to be a splendid opportunity for the enthusiastic theorist to observe the true cause of disaster. "We know he is going to miss it," we exclaim, "let us see whether he moves his body or takes his club back crooked, or his eye up too soon." Disappointment awaits us, for he appears to do none of these things, and we must conclude that T. Drummond missed a two-foot putt because T. Drummond did not hit the ball straight.

After that comes a most exciting picture, called "A Firm Putt by J. Milne." We see a blank green, with the hole near the audience. Next in the background a pair of boots slowly obtrude themselves, seeming, no doubt, owing to the eccentricities of photography, to be of colossal proportions. They are followed by the legs and club of J. Milne, who appears, bit by bit, like the Cheshire cat in *Alice in Wonderland*. He directs the ball towards the hole; it comes straight at the right-hand lip, and looks as if it must bob in and out of the hole, but no! the putt, having been termed by the management a firm putt, is resolved to justify its name, and by a supreme display of determination the ball just falls into the hole. Then J. Milne, his boots and his club flit away once more into the land of dreams and shadows, where live all those wonderful, unrecorded strokes that we are always going to make.

THE CURSE OF IMAGINATION

Some years ago there was an unfortunate gentleman who finished eighteen holes down in a team match. As the match was only one of eighteen holes, it was felt that in a record-breaking age there was at least one feat that was very unlikely to be beaten, and several comments appeared upon it in the newspapers. Thereupon the gentleman wrote a most pathetic letter, in which he complained, if I remember rightly, that two mitigating circumstances had not been mentioned: first, that he was playing with a strange set of clubs; and secondly, that he had only just recovered from a severe attack of influenza. Now here were two unimpeachable excuses. They were much better than most excuses, and yet it is hardly open to doubt that the gentleman would have done better to keep silence. It is a hard lesson—so hard that scarcely any of us learn it thoroughly—that not only do other people not care about our excuses, but they do not even believe them.

To all our adversary's excuses we make, if we are wise, one and the same answer, "Hard luck!" but in our own minds we do in a measure differentiate between them. The one to which we mentally extend the very smallest possible amount of sympathy is the excuse that the enemy's hand slipped, or, as it is sometimes stated with wholly unconvincing exaggeration, that "the club flew clean out of my hand." The proper answer to that remark is clearly, "Then why the dickens did you not hold tighter?" Everybody thinks it, though few are brutal enough to say it. The statement that the player's foot slipped is not looked upon with such scorn, because no doubt the best regulated feet will slip sometimes. Not infrequently, however, our feet slip just because they are not well regulated; because, in fact, we overswing ourselves in a very outrageous manner.

Then there is, of course, that enormous race of excuses that may be classed under the head of diseases. Now there is only one imperative piece of advice about diseases; we must remember to mention them before the game begins. There is everything to gain by this honest policy and nothing to lose, except, indeed, the character for suffering in Spartan silence, and that we have as a rule irretrievably lost long ago. A disease clearly announced on the first tee may possibly be believed in; and it may actually mitigate the shame of defeat or enhance the glories of a victory. The chances of a victory are always worth considering, because it is a common knowledge that a splitting headache, or, still better, a severe cold in the head, will sometimes lead to incredible brilliancy. On the other hand, a disease bottled up to begin with, and only brought out as a last resource when we are four down at the sixth hole is worse than useless. It will do no good if we lose, while if by some miracle we pull ourselves together and win, it will add an unspeakable bitterness to our enemy's ordinary discomfiture. He will probably not forget to mention to a few friends our mendacious and contemptible tactics.

There are numerous things which are recognised as being reasonably good excuses. Under this head come dogs, people standing or moving immediately behind us, and, commonest of all perhaps, caddies suffering from the hiccups. These are, as it were, excuses by Act of Parliament. Nobody would think of arguing about them, and we shall be quite safe in using them. The only question is whether it would not be better, after all, to refrain from doing all the law allows. When all is said, however, I think that by far the best excuse is a photographer. He stands and aims at us from a position that would in the cricket field be known as "silly point," and he keeps us on tenterhooks as to the exact moment at which he will apply the fuse to his infernal machine. As a rule, it is our classical follow-through that he desires to photograph, and so we can, at least, go through the subsidiary performance of hitting the ball in some kind of peace, but sometimes a not-unjustifiable fear seizes him that we are not going to follow through at all. Then, to make quite sure of bagging something, he fires just as we are coming down to the ball.

Never was any one so plagued with cameras as was Miss Leitch in her historic match against Mr. Hilton at Walton

Heath. Pale, but courageous, she had to play nearly every
shot under a heavy fire. When she got into difficulties the
fusillade was worst of all, snapping fiends posting themselves
actually on the very ramparts of the bunker. Mr. Hilton did
not have nearly such a trying time of it in this respect. He is,
I suppose, regularly kept in stock. His follow-through, his cap
tumbling off, his cigarette—all have been part of golfing
history so long that a good reliable picture can always be
obtained at a moment's notice. Through his many battles
on the links, he has been, as it were, inoculated against
photographers and enjoys a measure of immunity.

Differing slightly in kind from those excuses with which he
plagues his adversary are the consolations which the golfer
administers to himself; consolations founded as a rule upon
a train of reasoning that will not for a moment bear searching
analysis. For instance, what can be commoner than the following scene: A. and B. are on the tee about to drive off to a
short hole. A. has the honour, and foozles the shot so egregi-
ously that the ball topples into a bunker in front of his nose.
Thereupon B. lays his ball about a yard from the pin. But a
moment ago A. was furious and miserable, but now he picks
up his ball, quite serene and happy, and remarks: "Ah well—it
doesn't matter. I could never have done any good against a
two." If he is playing in a single he cheers himself by this
reflection; if in a foursome he expects to cheer his partner by
it.

How angry he would be, if his foursome partner were to
address him in some such words as these: "Do not talk such
arrant nonsense. If you had hit your ball over the bunker, not
only would B. not have put his ball dead, but I think it highly
probable that he would not have put it even on the green."
A player who should make such an observation would be
neither a popular nor a successful foursome player, but he
would have the barren satisfaction of feeling that he had, as
nearly as possible, spoken the truth. It is a truth that one
seldom hears openly acknowledged. Most golfers dislike it,
because to admit that the good or bad shots of other people
so often depend on circumstances that may be called mental
is also to admit a certain nervous weakness in themselves.
Therefore, we all join in a general conspiracy to deny the

obvious fact that we are all much more likely to play a good shot when our adversary is in a bunker than when he is lying dead at the hole.

I remember one honest man who declined to be a party to this conspiracy. He was complaining of his bad play, and in particular of how he had lost a certain hole in spite of having received a stroke there. I murmured that I had been very lucky at that hole, and got down a very long putt for a three. My friend refused to be consoled. "Yes, sir," he said, and his manner was worthy of Dr. Johnson, "but if I had put my third dead, as I ought, you would not have holed your long putt."

This kind of spurious consolation at any rate does little harm. It is rather contemptible, but it may stop us from getting angry. There is, however, another kind which is sometimes administered by an adversary which quite justifies us in striking him to the earth with a niblick. We are, let us imagine, playing a hole which, with a favouring breeze, we can reach very easily with a drive and an iron shot. We ought, therefore, to do a four, but, in fact, we do a five, a result with which we express ourselves as dissatisfied. There upon our offensive beast of an opponent says, "Oh well, it is a Bogey five." If I were on the jury in a trial for murder, and it was proved that this provocation had been given, nothing should induce me to find the prisoner guilty. What more deadly insult can there be than to insinuate that we cannot form our own estimate of the score in which we ought to do a hole; that we have to be instructed on that point by a half a dozen old gentlemen sitting in committee and imagining what an imaginary old gentleman would do.

A form of consolation, which has a substratum of sense underlying it, is often expressed in the words, "Well, anyhow, I hit the ball." True, the ball is at the bottom of the deepest bunker on the course, and the hole is hopelessly lost, but still——. In this case there is a distinction to be drawn as to the spirit in which we say the words. If we are merely arrogant, puffed up with the fact of hitting the ball farther than our opponent, although his ball is lying on the turf and ours in a bunker, then we are also silly, because the object of the game is to get into the hole in the smallest possible number of shots.

If, on the other hand, we rejoice only because that cleanly hit shot gives promise of future shots, which shall be hit not only clean but straight, then we are being moderately sensible. On this second ground it is sometimes almost cheering to begin a match with a fine long hit in the direction of long-on. A long hook generally means that we are at any rate getting well through with the shot. When we have warmed to our work, and the early morning stiffness has disappeared, we may reasonably hope that the length and the follow-through will remain and the hook disappear. In the same way it is endurable to start a round with a long putt in which the ball races past the hole, far out of holing distance. It is bad if it is going to frighten us and make us short for the rest of the round. It is good if we accept it merely as evidence that we are doing that most difficult thing, hitting the ball a fine, free blow with the middle of the putter.

Doubtless all these are but the idlest fancies, and we should do well to cast them from us. But there are few who have the strength of mind to fight their battles without some support, however illusory. There are at golf so many horrible things that we know are going to happen, and that do happen. There is the really appalling way in which history repeats itself in the matter of hazards. I do not know who originally remarked that "familiarity breeds contempt," but I do not believe he was a golfer. Rather does it too often breed an intolerable measure of respect. A year ago I spent a most delightful month at Ashdown Forest, and at the end of it I knew exactly what I was going to do at nearly every hole. I knew that I should push my first tee shot into the heather, and at the fourth hole hit my second far too gently and off the heel of the iron. At the dreaded "island" hole I should give a horrible lurch of my body, resulting either in an ineffectual sort of fluff or else in a half-topped skimmer which raced far over the green. At the twelfth I should hit the ball beautifully clean, and my follow-through would be much admired by anybody seeing me from afar off, but the ball would fly away to the left with the accuracy of a homing pigeon, ultimately to repose in a particular patch of bracken. Finally, at the fifteenth, I should pitch just too far; the ball would run down the sloping green into a rut, while I called gods and men to witness that it was a grossly unfair shot. Much as I loved Ashdown, I began to long for a course where the doctrine of predestination should not oppress me quite so heavily: where to get into a hazard should be an unpleasant surprise instead of being merely part of a daily routine. It is, of course, a dreadful mistake to be a fatalist at golf, but it is one dreadfully difficult to avoid. Consider the case of our match with Jones, whom for some reason we are particularly anxious to beat. We are both on the green in the same number of strokes. Jones plays the odd; he makes an execrable putt and runs some three or four yards past the hole. We feel practically certain that we have only to get dead in the like in order to win the hole. Let our ball be within two feet of the hole, and we will bet anything in reason that Jones makes a most miserable attempt for the half. We play, and we do not lay our ball dead. We do not make such a vile putt as he did, but we are several feet away from the hole. Nobody could possibly give us that putt; certainly not Jones, who is an ungenerous fellow, and likes his pound of flesh. The worst of it is that *now* it is absolutely certain that he will hole his four-yard putt. We may shut our eyes and buoy ourselves up by murmuring *sotto voce*, "He is sure to miss it." The rattle of his ball against the tin will soon undeceive us; not that we ever really were deceived, the thing was and is a certainty. Moreover, a similar tragedy befalls us in respect to bunkers. Jones puts his ball into a bunker. "We've got you this time," we say to ourselves, and, removing the eye too impetuously, deposit the ball in the very identical bunker. As we approach the bunker we observe that one ball is lying teed on a little pinnacle of sand; the other, what there is visible of it, is in a deep footmark in close proximity to a perpendicular black board. There is no need to inquire which ball is which. Of course, Jones is on the pinnacle. We knew he would be.

Golf is a horribly unforgiving game. We are told that "the cards never forgive," but the experience of a lamentable bridge player is that they are not half so relentless as golf clubs and balls. I was once upon a time playing in the semi-final of a certain handicap tournament. Going to the last hole, which was an easy one, I was dormy one down; my opponent had to receive a stroke, and he hit a good tee shot. A more depressing predicament from my point of view could not be conceived. As we were walking up to our respective balls the enemy remarked that he hoped his favourite driver, which had some ailment or other, would hold out for the final. At those words the fire of hope, which had almost gone out, absolutely flared up in my breast. Surely the golfing fates could never forgive a speech that flouted them so impudently. Nor did they forgive, for the rash man's second shot went plump into a bunker, he took three putts on the green, and neither he nor his driver played any part in the final of that tournament.

WITH IRON CLUBS

"Every player," says Sir Walter Simpson, "has a scheme of approaching known only to himself and his caddie." The first part of this statement is undeniably true; the second can only be so as regards a caddie who has carried the player's clubs many times. Yet how often, regardless of common sense, do we expect a small boy, who has never seen us play before, to understand the finest shades of distinction in our scheme of approaching, distinctions which would only be perceived by an intuitive genius amounting to second sight. Every one plays different shots with different clubs, and labels them with different names.

It is recorded as one of the guileful arts of Allan Robertson of illustrious memory that if his opponent had to play the odd he would call in an audible voice for the wrong club with intent to deceive. No doubt it was very wicked of Allan, but, if it was a question between one iron club and another, it was also very foolish of the opponent to be taken in, for one golfer's names for his approach shots can be of little use in guiding another. Most fallacious of all is the expression a "full mashie" in the mouth of any save those who know thoroughly our own particular scheme. Does it mean that the distance is the longest that can be compassed by using the ordinary comparatively short and restrained swing, or rather hit with the mashie, or does it mean that we are to whirl the club round one's head as one does with a driver, and play the stroke that Mr. Croome calls the "illegitimate shot with the iron"?—I don't know what he would call it if played with a mashie. It is the fact that many people make use of this full shot with a more or less lofted iron, and that others avoid it as they would the plague, that makes it so hard for one player to understand or be guided by another's scheme of approaching. Most great authorities tell us that we ought never, or practically never, to play full shots with irons; "the moment you begin to swing an iron you go wrong," is quoted as a maxim of Mr. Laidlay, who certainly speaks with authority. Whenever, therefore, we feel a temptation to play this full shot with an iron we are told that we should take a rather stronger club and play a half-shot with it. No doubt many of the finest iron players hardly ever do play more than a half-shot, though I am inclined to fancy that they play the "illegitimate" shot more often than they suppose; further, they have almost invariably very strong wrists and forearms, and for them it would be impertinent to suggest any other than their own scheme; but for the great mass of golfers I believe this advice as to half-shots to be something of a snare.

Most people who are not gifted with great strength of wrist and forearm find (at least, this is my personal experience) very great difficulty in hitting any considerable distance with a half-shot without the gravest danger of moving the body. There seems to be an irresistible inclination to lurch forward with the body in order to gain distance, although there is, in fact, no surer method of losing it; to us humbler ones it is easier to keep the balance steady and restrain the forward movement of the body by taking the full, or comparatively full, swing. This shot has, I think, another advantage for most people when playing down wind, or even on a calm day: they find it easier to get the ball well into the air with a full swing, and so can play boldly for the green with the hope of a comparatively dead fall. On the other hand, it is against the wind that we full swingers with the iron find out our weaknesses; then we envy—oh! how keenly—the man who can take a driving mashie or a very straight-faced iron and send the ball flying low and hard into the wind with a half-shot. As to the full shot with a mashie, that is only permissible down a wind; to try it against a wind is almost inevitably to court disaster.

While, then, we defend our "illegitimate" shot as being well suited to our humble powers and as being under certain conditions a really useful stroke, it will be fatal if we come to rely on it alone and do not cultivate some sort of push or half-shot—the name is immaterial. Many of the iron-swingers have a distinct hiatus in their approaching scheme, which lies between the gentlest of their full swinging strokes and their ordinary wrist stroke with a mashie. Sometimes they are lucky, and play several consecutive rounds without happening on a stroke over this their awkward distance; then luck will turn, and at hole after hole they will be confronted with a shot which is for them neither fish nor fowl. Having attempted a series of compromises and made a sad mess of them, they try and bridge over the gap by wildly purchasing approaching cleeks and "jiggers," but the gap will not be entirely bridged over. Therefore we must learn some kind of half-way-house shot which has to be played, as far as I understand the matter, a good deal with the right forearm. A friend of mine, a very good player and a ferocious critic, always reserves his bitterest contempt for those who cannot play this shot; the forearm push is, he declares, the most important factor in golf. Perhaps he exaggerates a little, but he is certainly right in so far as it is a bad thing to be without it altogether. Let us, then, cultivate it assiduously, but not wholly at the expense of our poor despised friend, the full shot with the iron.

This expression "push-shot" has now become so fashionable that it may mean almost anything; very often it only means that the player is trying to imitate Harry Vardon, and failing most signally to do so. Once upon a time we never used to hear of it at all, and to me it is still rather a puzzling term, or rather, perhaps, I am puzzled by the very varied uses to which it is put. I very often doubt whether I personally have ever played a push-shot proper in the whole course of my life. I remember once reading a report of a match, from the pen of a learned writer, in which I was described as having played a push-shot with a cleek up to the fifth hole. The stroke was associated with the most flattering epithets, but I was rather taken aback, because I had only been conscious of swinging my driving mashie as far and hitting the ball as hard as I possibly could. Equally, when I watch golf, I frequently fail to detect when a push-shot is being played. The first player in respect to whom I ever heard the term used was Mr. Mure Fergusson, and his push-shot I can detect. It seems to me to have been very happily christened. But in the case of other eminent persons I often think that a half shot is a better and more intelligible term. The distinction, at any rate, is as often

as not too subtle for me, and possibly a good many other
people would play better if they simplified their vocabulary
in this respect. For saying this, I have had to put up with some
contumelious abuse from a friendly critic. He tells me that
anybody who is not a hopeless imbecile can see from a range
of a hundred yards whether or not Mr. de Montmorency is
playing his push-shot or not. Well, I will give him that
redoubtable player; he certainly has a strongly marked
method, but, generally speaking, I adhere to my original
stupidity.

Another new term, which is rather misleading, though
admirable in itself, is the "dunch" shot, an expression, I
believe, only correctly used with regard to Braid. When one
has seen Braid play this particular stroke, "dunch" is rather
a good descriptive word; it is, indeed, almost onomatopœic.
It conveys the wonderful force wonderfully controlled, the
divot sent hurtling through the air, the ball tearing its un-
deviating way through a cross wind. But find a golfer who
has never seen Braid play: tell him that there is a shot called
the "dunch," and that he is to play the stroke suggested to
his mind by the sound of name. My impression is that he
would lift his club up high over his head and bury it in the
turf about two inches behind the ball; in other words, he
would play something very like the common niblick shot. On
the other hand, tell him to play a half-shot with a straight-
faced iron, taking care to keep his body under rigid control.
He will not play the stroke as well as Braid, but he will have
some sort of idea as to what he is to do. Dunching by ear, if
I may so term it, is dangerous work.

I don't know if any word has ever been coined to express
another tremendous shot, the half-shot with an iron club as
played by Mr. Maxwell. I doubt if there is any one word in
the language which is equal to the task, though possibly Mr.
Guy Ellis, who used to invent wonderful words for different
shots, could design one. I have said that with the ordinary and
incompetent person the great difficulty in playing a half-shot is
to prevent the body from lurching forward. Well, Mr.
Maxwell does not prevent it, he encourages the lurch and
glories in it. He hurls his by no means inconsiderable weight
forward with the concentrated ferocity of a battering ram and

away flies the ball, very low, very straight, and an unconscionable distance. It is the most alarming shot of a most alarming player.

The world "dunch" has, as I have said, a sound as of one frantically burying his club in the depths of a bunker, and so by a natural transition I come to the niblick. I do not speak of it as an approaching club, though nowadays the niblick does a good deal of delicate pitching in addition to the dirty work which is its natural lot. I speak of it in its original capacity of a very present help in trouble.

At a course with which I am well acquainted there was at one time no professional, and the foreman at a neighbouring carpenter's shop used to act as a sort of amateur-professional and impart some very elementary instruction to such scholars as he could get. His invariable practice was to put two or three balls in a narrow sandy drain on the way to the second hole and watch his pupils' ineffectual efforts to hack them out, for, he would say, "you are sure to get into many bunkers, and therefore the first thing to do is to learn to get out of them." It may be doubted whether such methods were calculated to attract learners, but that professor had at any rate grasped the fact that niblick play is an art, and not merely an inspiration.

It is not uncommon to hear a golfer who has made a deplorable muddle of an apparently simple shot in a bunker advance the singular excuse that the ball lay too well. This is a terrible confession of weakness, but it is a weakness to which many are subject, though they may know better than to admit it. There are, no doubt, greater possibilities in the way of a complete foozle, when the ball lies perfectly clean on smooth sand: even the very greatest can occasionally fluff these treacherous little shots, and Taylor, in his famous match in the final of the "News of the World" tournament against Robson, missed one at the tenth hole in the second round, that came near to costing him very dearly indeed. It is, however, a very rare mistake with a professional, and there is nothing, I am inclined to think, in which he more clearly excels the amateur than in this art of chipping a clean-lying ball out of a bunker. Even the humbler professional, the rest of whose game inspires no particular awe, is usually a past master of this shot, perhaps because in his younger days he was for ever illicitly chipping about with his master's mashie on the broken and sandy country around the caddies' shed. It appears to me—and I speak as a confirmed fluffer—that most people in playing the shot take the club too straight up and down, under an exaggerated idea of the necessity of picking up the ball. To play thus demands the genius of Massy, who plays all his short pitches with an extraordinarily abrupt lift of the club. It is a fascinating style, but woe be to its imitator, for the slightest inaccuracy means certain disaster. A flatter stroke, in which the clubhead travels near the surface of the sand as long as possible, seems to allow a larger margin of error. The ball may not be hit quite clean, and yet be scuffled out of the bunker somehow.

Most of us beyond doubt are rather afraid of these clean-lying balls in bunkers, and feel more comfortable when we can take a whole-hearted slog into the sand behind the ball and explode it out rather than hit it. But when the hole is too far from the bunker for us to be able to gauge the force of our explosion with any nicety, we have to harden our hearts and take the ball clean, and a horrid business it is, made the more aggravating by our opponent's audible grumbles that we have got a teed ball when we ought to be up to our neck in sand. On the other hand, we must never think that if the ball lies clean in a bunker it is our bounden duty to hit it clean, regardless of circumstances. To do so, when the bunker is quite close to the hole, is not as a rule the act of a wise man; rather must we take a prodigious lot of sand, so that the force of the explosion is nearly spent by the time it reaches the ball, but is just sufficient to drop it limply on the green. It is extraordinary how often this shot, if we play it properly, lays the ball dead, or nearly so, but as a rule we fall into what Mr. Bob Sawyer, though not in allusion to sand, called "the vulgar error of not taking enough."

No doubt the sight of the ball lying cleanly makes it more difficult to refrain from hitting it first and the sand afterwards, but even with a badly lying ball in a bunker to top is the most frequent of errors. Braid says that most people make the mistake of not standing far enough behind the ball. Perhaps the idea of coming straight down is too predominant in our minds, and we stand too much over it in order to chop the harder, but probably all these various errors that can be made in a bunker are neither so serious nor so frequent as the simple one of removing the eye from the ball. That is always with us.

More difficult and important than either of the shots I have mentioned is, as I at least believe, the bunker shot which lies midway between the two. It is what may be called a half-shot with the niblick, when the ball does not lie clean enough for us merely to flick it out, and yet there is no pressing reason for our hitting as hard as we can. To be sure we can get over our difficulties by playing a shot of a volcanic type and regulating with infinite precision the distance we hit behind the ball; but this is not the way of the masters of the niblick, so far as I have observed them. No, they hit moderately hard with a comparatively short swing of the club, kept well under control. In fact, it is a half-shot, and just as the half-shot, when the ball lies upon turf, is one of the standing tests of a golfer, so this half-way shot out of sand finds out the weakness of many of us.

Mr. Low, who knows as much about the use of the niblick as any one—not, I hasten to add, from compulsory experience but from voluntary study—tells us that "a light niblick is of little use in sand, or, at any rate, its use is narrowed down to one shot—the full smack or dig." It is comforting to think that some of our lack of skill comes from our niblick being an insufficiently formidable bludgeon, but I am afraid that does not wholly account for it. No doubt, however, Mr. Low is quite right, and a great many niblicks are neither heavy enough nor lofted enough. Naturally, if one wants the very latest word in any particular kind of club, one flies to the unequalled collection of Mr. H. E. Taylor, and Mr. Taylor has in his bag a magnificent specimen of the niblick. It has a shaft like the mast of a ship, and is so tremendously lofted that the blade appears to be lying on its back staring straight up to heaven. It is a king amongst niblicks, and belongs to that race which Mr. Low describes as "sonsy-faced, saucer-countenanced billies, of which no man need be ashamed even to be observed in handshake."

There is one piece of advice as to niblick play in scoring

competitions which can be backed up by an historical instance. It is, never to forget, in the agony of the moment, that
you are entitled to tee and lose two shots. In the St. George's
Cup of 1898 Mr. Hutchinson led the field comfortably in the
morning, and was doing well in the second round till his ball
got embedded in the black timber terraces on the face of the
Maiden. I should be sorry to state how many he took to the
hole, but I know that he declared afterwards that he had quite
forgotten that there was any possible alternative to hacking
the ball grimly out. It certainly was one of life's little ironies
that such a disaster should befall one who must know, if any
man does, the rules of golf, and who is also, as far as
my experience goes, the most accomplished player out of
difficulties in the world.

To say that is high praise, but I am sure that I have
never seen any one who had such ingenious methods of
getting out of trouble or such an infinity of resource. There
are few golfing gifts of which I feel more envious than that
one. The advantage that a really great player can gain in
bunker play, presuming that the bunkers are not made so
impossibly vindictive as to reduce all players to the dead
level of the "common thud," is wonderful. The mere
certainty of their getting the ball out, if it is humanly
possible, is a great asset, but they do much more than that:
they put it on the green; they not infrequently lay it dead.
We others need not aspire to such diabolic excellence as
that, but we should like to have such a degree of skill with
the niblick as not to be unduly terrified of bunkers.

We should drive all the straighter for not being frightened;
we should go more successfully for a long carry because our
hearts were lighter. We might be reformed and regenerated
altogether, if we would only practise with the niblick; but
that is just what we will not do. Some while ago the powers
that be at Walton Heath conceived the luminous idea of
making practice bunkers instead of the usual practice putting-
greens in front of the club-house. No doubt, the bunkers were
well worth the getting out of, for Mr. Fowler's skill in making
them is only equalled by his ferocity, but apparently there
were but few students of the niblick whose enthusiasm enabled
them to bear the inevitable flood of ribald merriment from

the club verandah, since the bunkers have now vanished and turf reigns in their stead.

For that matter, to strike a ball through a fusillade of deliberate and provocative shouts is really a difficult matter. I was once playing a foursome at Woking, and by the ninth green, which lies close to the high-road, we came across an army of fifty or sixty small boys, the inmates of a home, or, as I should imagine from their conduct, a reformatory. We succeeded in holing out through a storm of cries, such as "Well played, Oxford!" and "Now then, Eton!" but when we got on to the tenth tee the whole body began to shout in a measured and imposing cadence, "One—two—three." The "one—two" for the waggle was not so bad, but to know that a stentorian "three" would come at the exact moment of hitting the ball was really paralysing. Having once before experienced the same treatment on another course from two partially intoxicated old ladies, I managed, by a miracle, to strike the ball with the middle of the club—indeed, it was one of the few I did so strike that afternoon; but our adversaries' ball took refuge in the nearest bunker, where they had ample opportunity of practising those varieties of the niblick shot that I have so laboriously described.

SOME COMMON REMEDIES

I am tempted to add one more chapter to deal with what I may call rule-of-thumb remedies for the commoner maladies of golfing childhood. In doing so I am going perhaps a little beyond the task I set myself. Properly considered, the beginner at golf has no definite maladies and his troubles are all before him; they will come upon him quickly enough, and one has no desire unduly to anticipate them. In the language of those who are wise in the bringing up of young persons, one does not want to "put things" in the child's head, and the golfing beginner ought not to be too prone to search for the cause of his failures. A certain number of them he must accept as resulting from the sufficiently obvious fact that he has never played golf before, and the best thing he can do is, in Sir Walter Simpson's words, to "aim more carefully." At the same time, after the ball has flown obstinately to the right or left, as the case may be, or trickled along the ground, or spouted feebly into the air a good many times in succession, he cannot be expected to close his eyes to the fact that the constantly repeated error arises from some particular fault.

Now there are certain faults which can only be cured in the most obvious way, namely, by trying to avoid them. For example, if a man be conscious of leaping, figuratively speaking, into the air at the top of his swing, and so of being far too much on his toes, I know of no remedy, save that he must try not to jump; he must peg his feet down by dint of sheer determination. But there are certain other common faults for which the accumulated wisdom of generations of golfers has discovered specific remedies for which this much may be said, that they very often have a beneficial effect. To mention just a few of these may be to do the learner a service. Most of them may very likely be of no use, but just one may prove a short cut whereby a certain amount of anguish may be avoided.

I begin with driving, and I suppose that by far the commonest of faults in driving is that of slicing. As soon as the learner has succeeded in getting the ball into the air, it is very likely to fly not straight, but in a highly irritating curve to the right. This unpleasant result may be produced in a number of ways; the disease cannot with any kind of certainty be diagnosed without seeing the patient, but the most usual cause is correctly stated in the drone of the professional teacher, "You're pulling in your arms." It is one thing to know that you are pulling in your arms, and quite another to avoid it, but there is one "tip" which I venture to think a good one. This is, that the patient should take great pains to see that his right arm brushes against his side as he brings the club down. Let him harden his heart and try to give himself a severe dig in the ribs with his right elbow. As I have stated, the up-swing is infinitely the most important thing. I will go a step further back and say, "Take pains that your right arm brushes your side both in the up swing and the down swing." Let any one stand up and try this kind of swing if necessary with the fire-irons. He will find it very difficult to pull his arms inwards and to the left of his body, because his body gets, so to speak, in the way of his arms and shoots them out to the right, whether they like it or not.

To the fault of topping, I hesitate to say anything at all, save that is an essential thing in golf to see the ball at the moment of striking it. Yet there is just one little bit of advice that may be given. It is, though only in aggravated cases, worth while ascertaining whether you have gradually and unconsciously fallen into a habit of having the ball in the wrong place relative to your feet. There are two ways in which you may be topping. The club-head may be reaching the lowest point in its swing before it ever reaches the ball, so that it ultimately hits the ball when on its upward path, and, if one may say so, scalps it. On the other hand, it may reach the ball before it has reached the lowest point of the swing, when, so far as in it lies, it drives the ball into the ground. In the first case, you have probably, or at any rate possibly, got the ball too far forward; in the second case, too far back.

The opposite of topping is "sclaffing," that is to say, hitting into the ground behind the ball, causing the destruction of the turf and an exceedingly feeble, spouting flight of the ball. Here, again, there may be many causes and many remedies of which I will only indicate two. You should, in the first place, remember that which you have perhaps allowed yourself to forget, that it is the club and not you that does the lofting. Take particular care to avoid any digging or delving or curtseying movements, such as have been mentioned before. In giving my second "tip" I am doing little more than drawing a bow at a venture. It is always worth while trying the effect of holding the club rather tighter. A limp and feeble grip does often lead to sclaffing. It may have nothing to do with it in your particular case, but at any rate there is little harm in trying, because the beginner is more likely to let go of his club than to hold it too tight.

Finally, as to what has been called general debility in driving. When the ball appears to be hit correctly and yet goes a wholly paltry and contemptible distance, it is wise to make sure that you are not standing a little nearer to the ball than you were. The vice of standing too near the ball often brings a number of others in its train, and here again you cannot do much harm in trying, since it is far easier even for the finished golfer to stand too near to his ball, rather than too far from it. As for the beginner, who feels frightened of missing the ball altogether if he does not keep close to it, he practically never stands too far away. There are, of course, hundreds more faults in driving which it is possible to commit, but I have no desire to turn the beginner into that most miserable creature, a fault-searching maniac, and so no more of driving, but just a few more words on iron play.

There is one fault—nay, it is not merely a fault—it is a disease, a scourge, a pestilence, to which all golfers whether of high or low degree are occasionally prone, and that is "socketing." It can be in a measure, of course, avoided by the expedient of using a club without a socket, one of those hideous, crooked-necked creations of Mr. G. F. Smith, which have so far escaped the legislative fervour of the Rules Committee. But this club, though it may mitigate the appalling nature of the consequences, cannot do away with the disease, namely the hitting of the ball on the extreme heel of the club, and whatever the weapon used, the disease is the most completely paralysing one known. A good general cure is to take back the club slowly, ludicrously slowly as it will at first seem to the player, who has perhaps got into a habit of snatching back his club at lightning speed. This, however, is not always sufficiently drastic, and then comes the time for the remedy which I call Mr. Charles Hutchings' remedy, because it was he who told me of it. I give it in his own words: "Rip the club right through with the right hand," and I do not think that I can improve on them by any explanation. This is a piece of teaching which is diametrically opposed to that of other people, who have declared that socketing proceeds from too vigorous a use of the right hand in bringing down the club. I cannot reconcile the two. I can only boldly state that I believe Mr. Hutchings to be right, and the other people wrong.

Putting is so largely a matter of mood and confidence, although a good deal also depends on art and method, that it is perhaps overbold to suggest remedies other than mental remedies. However, I will hazard two small "tips." If the player finds he is never hitting his putts properly, and cleanly—and to hit a putt cleanly is not an easy thing to do—it is a good plan to address the ball with the extreme nose of the putter and to try to hit it there. The reason, I take it, is that there is a fatally common inclination to hit putts off the heel of the club, while at the same time it is quite a frequent occurrence to commit this crime throughout a whole round without discovering it; therefore it is always worth while to try the nose of the club.

The commonest of all putting faults is undoubtedly that of being short. In this the remedy at first sight seems too obvious to mention. What remedy can there be, the reader may well ask, save that of hitting the ball harder? That is, to be sure, the best one, and yet there are occasions when, in spite of the most savage resolutions on the part of the striker, the ball will not go up to the hole. Then the old Scottish caddie will say to him, "Tak' a firm grip of your putter"—and that with a formidable rolling of the *r* in firm. It is a good sound piece of advice, because when we are always short, we are nearly always frightened, and when we are frightened, we are exceedingly apt to let the putter fall from our hands.

ABERDOVEY

The golfer is often said to be a selfish person. He deserts his wife for days together; he objects to the presence of bank-holiday makers upon the common, where he desires to play his game; he commits various other crimes. He is almost certainly selfish about the festival of Christmas, in that the kind of Christmas which other people want is to him hateful beyond words. For the Christmas which English people are at any rate supposed to enjoy there are necessary, besides mistletoe and plum pudding, which do no one any harm, a fall of snow and a good hard frost—two things which, it is superfluous to observe, are wholly inimical to golf. The golfer likes to read of the typical "old-fashioned" Christmas, such as Caldecott drew, or Dickens described, but in reading he likes to translate it, as it were, into his own terms.

For instance, one of the most delightful pieces of literature in the world, and the one most redolent of Christmas, is the account of the Pickwickians' journey by the Muggleton coach, on their way to Dingley Dell. There is Mr. Pickwick watching the "implacable" codfish squeezed into the boot: Mr. Pickwick begging the guard to drink his health in a glass of hot brandy and water: the horses cantering, and the wheels skimming over the hard and frosty ground: the meeting with the fat boy who had been asleep "right in front of the tap-room fire." All these things are perfectly heavenly, but it is one of the disadvantages of having a mind warped by golf that one cannot help remembering that this journey was a prelude to Mr. Winkle's skating and Mr. Pickwick's sliding, and where there is ice, there is no golf worthy of the name. So I have to translate this glorious journey to myself into my own language. It may sound lamentably prosaic; there will be no cracking of whips and tooting of horns, but this journey of mine is good to look forward to, nevertheless.

Before the journey comes the packing, a thing usually loathsome, but on this occasion positively delicious, more especially the packing of clubs. All the clubs are taken out one by one, looked at with a gloating eye, and then stowed triumphantly into the bag. Of course, I shall take more than I really want, just for the fun of packing them. There are one or two wooden clubs from my reserve which must certainly go. There is one brassy that only wants just a drop of lead let into the head to make it an enchanter's wand. There is an iron that I have not used for some time that will be just the thing for carrying the mighty sandhill, crowned with ominous sleepers, that guards the fourth green; and then, of course, one must take a spare putter or two, against the almost unthinkable event of going off one's putting. Also there is a large umbrella, though it can never be that the fates will be so unkind as to make one use it.

So much for the packing, and now for the journey, which will begin, not in a coach, but in a cab, which will take me to Euston, most dear and romantic of stations. I shall instruct a porter as to the label to be affixed to my bag, adding quite unnecessarily, but with an additional thrill of joy, "On the Cambrian Railway, you know." I shall not ask him to drink my health in brandy and water, but in the enthusiasm of the moment I shall probably give him sixpence. I shall take my seat in the carriage and that almost certainly a corner seat, because in my excitement I shall have reached the station absurdly early. Then I shall start. I shall not read the paper that I have bought, because I shall be looking out of the window at the golf courses that I pass on my way and thinking, without any disrespect to them, how far pleasanter is the course to which I am bound.

The stations will whirl past. Bletchley, Rugby, Stafford, Wellington, and at last beloved Shrewsbury. So far I shall have been alone, but at Shrewsbury will be encountered my two kind hosts and other golfers bound for the same paradise. We shall greet each other uproariously, behaving in an abominably hearty and Christmas-like way, and then we shall pack ourselves into another carriage, for the second half of our journey. Our talk, surprising as it may appear, will be about the game of golf—whether there is casual water in the

Crater green, and how many of the new bunkers have been made. I should not be surprised if we even attempted to waggle each other's clubs in the extremely confined space at our disposal.

More stations will go by us. They will not whirl this time, for the trains from Shrewsbury to Wales are not given to whirling; they will pass in leisurely order. Hanwood, Westbury, and now the Welsh border is crossed; Buttington, Welshpool, Abermule, Montgomery, Newtown—I forget their order, but love to write down their names. The train comes into a country of mountains and jolly, foaming, mountain streams; it pants up a steep hill to a solitary little station called Talerddig. Near Talerddig there is a certain mysterious natural arch in the rock, and it is a point of honour with us to look for it out of the window. However, since we never can remember exactly where it is, and the twilight is deepening, we never see it. Now the train has reached the end of its painful climb, and dashes down the hill into the valley, and by this time we feel as if we could almost smell the sea. There is a pause at Machynlleth (let any Saxon try to pronounce that!), and we have tea and listen to the people talking Welsh upon the platform. Then on again through the darkness, till we stop once more. There is a wild rush of small boys outside our carriage window, fighting and clamouring for the privilege of carrying our clubs. *Nunc dimittis*—we have arrived at Aberdovey.

Escaping with difficulty from this rabble of boys, we clamber up a steep and rocky road to where our house stands, perched upon the hillside, looking out over the estuary and at the lights of Borth that twinkle across the water. We have our annual argument with an old retainer of Scottish ancestry and pedantically exact mind, who points out to us that it is clearly impossible that we should all be called at precisely eight o'clock in the morning. We suggest as a compromise that one should be called at two minutes to eight, and another at two minutes past, and to this course, though still unconvinced, he grudgingly assents. Then next day, when the hour of calling has come, we wake, if all is well, to one of the most seraphic of imaginable winter days, for be it known that Aberdovey is called by the local guide-book the Madeira of

North Wales, and that one hardy schoolmaster played there on two successive New Year's days in his shirt sleeves. Warm, still and grey, with no dancing shadows to distract the more fanciful of our party—that is how I like it best, and that is how, in a good hour be it spoken, it generally is. Yet there are exceptions, and I remember almost painfully well one Christmas, when it was indeed a "fine time for them as is well wropped up." This, it will be remembered, was the soliloquy of the polar bear when he was practising his skating, and we who were practising our golfing heartily endorsed the reflections of that arctic philosopher. Yet even so we played our two rounds a day like men, and that says something both for us and for Aberdovey.

The ground was iron hard with frost, the east wind blew remorselessly, and we were certainly very well wrapped up indeed. Spartan persons who had never yielded before were glad to nestle inside Shetland waistcoats, while at the same time reluctantly admitting that mittens did restore some vestige of feeling to the fingers. It is indeed dreadful to contemplate life in winter-time without that blessed invention the mitten, or, to give it its technical name, the muffetee. A mitten proper has a hole for one's thumb, and so comes too far over the palm of the hand to allow a comfortable grip of the club. The muffetee, which is made of silk, if one is extravagant, and of wool, if one is economical, only encircles the wrist with a delicious warmth that in a surprisingly short space of time permeates the wearer's entire frame.

There are still a good many people who will not believe that this is so. I have come across this wilful blindness among my own relations, who are of a highly scientific and sceptical turn of mind. They allege the most futile and irrebuttable reasons why the warmth of the wrist should have no connection with the warmth of the hand, but there is a measure of consolation in the fact that they suffer agonies from cold fingers, and, better still, top their mashie shots in consequence. Of course, when they have once tried the experiment they have to give in and own churlishly enough that there seems to be something in it. Even the most distinguished of golfers are sometimes to be caught without mittens. I have twice played the part of Sir Philip Sidney and lent mine to eminent professionals when they were playing quite important matches on the most bitterly cold days. Those that I lent to Taylor were, needless to say, returned to me permanently enlarged, and ever afterwards hung loosely upon my puny and attenuated wrists. If, however, they are no longer very useful as mittens, they are as precious to me as were the three cherry stones to Calverley's young lady, from having "once dallied with the teeth of royalty itself."

I believe that there is a Brobdingnagian kind of mitten to be bought which reaches from the wrist to the elbow. I have never yet had a pair, but some day I shall certainly try to afford one. Meanwhile, the ordinary woollen mitten is within the reach of all, since a pair costs, if I remember rightly, no more than sevenpence halfpenny. They will do more towards winning you your winter half-crowns than all the curly-necked clubs in the world, or even, I suspect, than the patent putter for which the advertisement used to claim that it "made every stroke practically a certainty."

This rhapsody on mittens has carried me far away from Aberdovey, where we were left battling with the elements. It is a curious game, that golf on frozen ground and in an easterly gale, for one reason because, after a few days of it, it is hard to remain entirely level-headed about our driving powers. The ball goes such portentous distances that we really cannot believe that it is entirely attributable to the weather. In our heart of hearts we half believe that some subtle change has come over us, and that we shall drive just a little farther ever afterwards. Thus, when we came in to lunch after our morning round—and oh! how good lunch was—we each had our little boast of some green reached, some bunker passed. We fully appreciated that the shots of others were mere accidents due to the ball falling upon a particularly frozen spot; but as to our own, there must have been just a little extra sting behind those—we thought we detected a new and wonderful use of our wrists that accounted for it.

Needless to say, at that Christmas time of bitter memory the obdurate wind took a rest on Sunday, as did the golfers. There was a cloudless day, without a breath of wind; we could have kept quite warm, and our approach shots would not have skipped like young rams upon the green, ere they buried themselves in a bunker fifty yards beyond it. All we could do was to bemoan our luck, and look at the view, a very beautiful one truly, for the Dovey estuary on a fine winter's day can show hills and woods and bracken as lovely as may be. Then one round in the thaw on Monday morning, just to rub it in that we were going to leave the course at its best, and so home to a singularly depressing London of slush and drizzle.

I have written of Aberdovey in winter because it is then, I think, that it is at its best, perhaps because I love it so much that I selfishly like to have it to myself. It is good in summer-time too; good even in August when the rain too often comes pitilessly down, when the hand of the great midland towns lies heavy on the course and a pitched battle rages daily between the outgoing and incoming battalions in the narrow space that lies between the Pulpit and the Crater hole. September is a divine month there, when there are but few people left, and so is June, when there are none at all. It was in June that I paid my last summer visit there, and that on a somewhat sacrilegious errand, for I was to aid in the altering of old holes and the making of new bunkers. The committee had decided to call in a highly distinguished golfing architect to set their house in order, and I was asked to attend him as *amicus curiæ* or bottle-holder, or clerk of the works—in short, in a menial capacity of an indefinite character. This task I undertook with alacrity, but after the first day's work I was a physical and mental wreck and felt a positive loathing for my architectural friend. Yet this I must say for him; like Rogue Riderhood, he does "Earn his living by the sweat of his brow." I never saw any one work harder. Save for a wholly insufficient interval for lunch, we were on our legs from 9.15 in the morning to 7.30 at night. As a warning to others who may lightly undertake this kind of work, even at the risk of too wide a digression, I will shortly describe our day.

We started out first of all with two caddies. One of them carried our two waterproofs and a large plan of the course nailed on to a board. The other carried my clubs. The architect himself did not take any clubs, but stated that I should hit balls for him when required. My sensations rather resembled, as I should imagine, those of one who accompanies a water diviner. The architect behaved in the same mysterious and interesting manner. Sometimes he would come to a full stop and remain buried in thought for no ostensible reason. Then he would suddenly turn round and retrace his steps to the tee. Then he would pace a certain distance, counting his paces aloud in a solemn manner. Finally he would give a cry of joy, make a dash up to the top of a little sandhill, and declare with triumph that it would make the most perfect plateau green in the world, and that why in the world those who had originally laid out the course had not discovered it he for one could not conceive.

By slow stages the first two holes, which the members had always considered rather good in a humble way, were completely transmogrified. The greens were moved in the architect's mind's eye from their then reasonably open and easy-going positions to the most devilish little narrow gullies surrounded by sandhills and bents, where only a ball that flies as straight as did an arrow from the bow of Robin Hood might hope to reach the green. Beautiful holes they were, both of them, and would make a magnificent beginning to the course, but I could not but feel an uneasy doubt as to whether all the long-handicap members of the club would appreciate them at quite their true value. Nothing much happened at the third hole, and then we approached the fourth, over which I personally felt rather nervous. The club is proud of this fourth hole, which consists of a rather terrifying iron shot, perfectly blind, over a vast and formidable hill shored up with black railway sleepers, on to a little green oasis amid a desert of sand. Now, the hole is really a sacred institution (it is one of the few holes on the course that is known by a name and not a number), but it is also one of the type of hole for which I knew my architect to feel a most utter contempt. I wondered uneasily whether he would want to do some horribly revolutionary thing, and I reflected that if he did I should certainly be lynched by the committee for his sins. However, he merely cast a withering look at a grass bank behind the green, commanded that "that back wall" should be taken away, and passed on, deeming the hole unworthy of any further notice. I will not enter into further details of this our first progress round the course. At intervals I was ordered to drive a ball from a specified place, and my efforts were commended as being admirably adapted for showing where the normal, short, bad driver would get to against the wind: this when I was driving with a fairly strong breeze behind me. To cut a long story short, we finally got round in something over three hours, and fell ravenously on our lunch.

I had faintly hoped that in the afternoon we might relax our labours so far as to play a friendly round, but as a matter of fact, what I had undergone in the morning was the merest child's play to the afternoon. After lunch we started out again with a large cart driven by a sleepy boy, and pulled by a sleepy horse. In the cart were about 200 stakes, commandeered from a neighbouring sawmill, for the purpose of marking the sites of proposed new bunkers. We started about 2.30, and we stopped about 6.30, and I cannot help thinking that those two small caddies who hammered in stakes with violent blows and a heavy mallet, must have been very stiff after their labours. Personally I grew infinitely more faint and weary than I have ever done even at a picture gallery, which is generally believed to be the most exhausting thing in the world. To give the devil his due, my architect was wonderful, and filled me with admiration. Like a comet, he left a shining tail behind him—of white stakes gleaming in the sunlight. The speed with which he would decide on the position of a bunker was really astounding. While I was feebly wondering what a certain stake was for, he had decided that the right policy was to make people play at the green from the right-hand side: to make a series of bunkers all along the left of the fairway so as to drive them towards the rushes: to dig out that hollow close to the green, and so on, and so on. He is really a wonderful person, but it is a fearful thing to do a day's work with him, even though it be in the service of the course one loves best in the world.

WINTER RULES

I should like to begin by making two dogmatic statements. The first is that golf is played for fun, and that is surely incontestable. The second is that it is not fun to hack the ball out of a wet, muddy hole with the risk of some of the mud spurting into your eye. This second statement may be contested because there are a good many people who play this sort of golf during a number of their winter week-ends, and they must be presumed to enjoy it or else they would not do it. I know that there was a time when I enjoyed it myself, for in enthusiastic youth I played many rounds on what I believe to have been the two muddiest courses in the civilised world, one the Athens course at Eton, and the other that at Coldham Common, Cambridge. Since then I have become spoilt and pampered by sand and heather, and the other day, when I played on real mud, with the addition, to be sure, of a yellow fog and a drizzling rain, I thought it a wholly odious occupation.

If we are going to play really muddy golf, then I believe it would be infinitely better fun if we teed, or, at any rate, placed, the ball whenever we had the mind to it. It may be said that to do so is a travesty of the game, but then golf on a mud-heap is a travesty in itself, and the great thing is to render it as agreeable as possible and as little destructive as possible to the turf. I very much doubt whether there is any educational advantage in playing strokes out of bad lies on a muddy course. Far from improving a man's golf, it is likely to inculcate the worst of habits by causing him to shut his eyes at the critical moment lest he be blinded with mud.

Holding, as I do, these atrocious and unorthodox sentiments, I was delighted to be told by a friend the other day that at his club during the winter months people habitually permitted themselves to place the ball through the green. I do not name the club, although I feel the highest admiration for the wisdom of its members. I have a great respect for the law of libel and, moreover, golfers are funny people; while liking their wisdom to be admired, they dislike any allusion to the very obvious fact that the soil of their course is unmitigated clay.

In America, where the official golfing season comes to an end with the first approach of winter, I believe that golfers regularly play "winter rules," that is to say, they pick up and place the ball whenever they like. Some time ago I met a distinguished friend who had just come back from a visit of six weeks or so in America. I did not ask him for his views on prohibition, or war debts, or Mr. Al Capone, though doubtless they would have been most illuminating. My first remark to him was: "Did you play winter rules?" He answered that he had, although this winter the weather had been so kind, and the courses near New York consequently in such good order, that such rules had really not been necessary. He had often found himself forgetting to avail himself of the placing privilege because his lie was a perfectly good one.

This method of playing the game in the United States is, of course, quite unofficial, and it is needless, I hope, to observe that I am not asking that august body the Rules of Golf Committee to make for us a code of winter rules. I am only suggesting to those who have perforce to play their winter games on mud that this is a gloriously free country, that nobody can stop them from placing their ball in a respectable lie instead of hewing it out of a bog, and that they will have better fun if they do. I would go even farther. If they like actually to tee the ball on a peg tee (which is a pleasanter and cleaner thing than a neighbouring wormcast) why shouldn't they do it? I once knew an old lady who regularly allowed herself three cheats, as she called them, in her game of patience, and enjoyed it the more accordingly. Equally enjoyable would be a few illicitly teed brassy shots. When a course, which may be going to be a very good one, is quite new, players are encouraged to tee the ball through the green, not so much for their own sake as the course's. On courses which are destined to be, in the winter, always very bad I would encourage in private games the same procedure. It would hardly do in competitions, but then it is a grave question whether competitions are worth playing on mud—I mean the real, rich, deep, black, oozy and glutinous article.

I began this paper by saying that we played golf for fun. So we do, and we are often ashamed of confessing what in our heart of hearts we think is the best fun. Some years ago I was driving from Walton Heath to Tadworth Station in a pleasantly drowsy fly with three other golfers. Three of us, who knew each other, were discussing the various beauties and difficulties of that great course, and were being, I dare say, extremely tiresome. After a while the fourth man, whom we had never met before, suddenly broke silence with the remark: "Don't you think it's a great deal too difficult?" Then, before we had recovered our breath, he added: "I have just been playing on the perfect golf course. It had no rough of any sort at all." Was he trying to pull our highly respectable legs? I think he was, though he kept a very grave face. We deserved it, too, for our rather solemn and priggish conversation: and, incidentally, it is as easy to be a prig about golf as about any other subject. At the same time, he more than half meant what he said, and we should hear the same thing said much oftener if there were many such honest men in the world. There is one course which used to answer exactly to his description. It is one of which I am very fond and I have often sung its praises before—Royston in Hertfordshire. Once upon a time there was no rough—not a particle—on all that splendid heath; one could hit the ball to square leg or over extra cover's head, and unless it went into a wood or a road, it always lay on the same delightful, springy down turf. Then something happened in the War-time—I have never clearly discovered what—and a certain amount of rough arose. When rough once comes it apparently stays, and one of the unique qualities of the course has gone. I still love it, but I confess to a feeling of almost intolerable grievance when an erratic stroke lands me, no doubt quite deservedly, in heavy grass. It was such a joy to know that one could *not* get into anything, and, as a result, one generally drove as straight as an arrow. Royston is still a fine restorer of confidence for anyone who has been too much cramped and confined amid lines of fir trees and heather, but, regarded simply as a cure, it is not quite what it was. Just a little of one particular kind of fun has departed, but the wind on the heath, that "makes you feel what a sweet thing it is to be alive"—that will always be there, thank goodness!

THE SOUNDS OF GOLF

In golf, as in everything else, there are certain characteristic sounds with which our ears grow familiar. We know them so well that we hardly realise their existence until we hear them again after an absence from the links or until, owing to some change in the game, we come to miss them. To these old familiar golfing sounds a new one has been added in the course of the last few years. It is the metallic clank caused by one steel shaft touching another as the caddie takes a club out of the bag. Perhaps clank is not quite the right word, for there is also something of purring in the sound. At any rate, though my vocabulary is vague and inadequate, the sound is perfectly distinct, and we shall soon know it so well that we shall hardly notice it any more than we do the roar of an aeroplane which once set us staring at the heavens.

For myself I first noticed it while playing in a foursome, all four members of which had gone worshipping after the strange new gods of steel. It set me trying to enumerate the other sounds characteristic of our game. Steel may fairly be said, I think, to have added another new one in the unmistakable "swish" of the shaft through the air. I have already grown accustomed to it, but when I first bought a particularly engaging little spoon, its music seemed infinitely exciting and romantic. Old Tom Morris used to talk of the music of a shaft, meaning the spring or whip in it. It was a charming and poetical thought which has now come to be a comparatively prosaic and everyday fact. It is comforting that the modern game should bring some pleasant sound with it, because the old game had beautiful ones that are now gone for ever. Some melody went out of golf when the rubber-core replaced the gutty. The ring of a gutty struck quite cleanly with an iron club was a twofold joy; it was cheerful and pretty in itself and spoke of a stroke perfectly made. It is only when we play a shot with a gutty and hear it again that we realise what we have lost. The gutty rang even off an iron putter. I have a feeling—no doubt quite fantastic and due to ancient hero worship—that the ball struck by that lofted putting cleek of Freddie Tait's sang a clearer, louder song than anyone else's. I am sure that one did know instantly and certainly whether a putt had been struck or not, and on rare red letter days one felt sure the ball was going down merely from the click with which it left one's club.

"Crack after crack rings out cleanly as every ounce of youthful muscle is thrown into the blow." I quote from memory, but I trust with reasonable accuracy, a passage which I love in Mr. Hutchinson's description of the young professionals and university students driving off at St. Andrews while Old Tom looks on to see that they do not trespass on the home green. That was written of the gutty, which I am prepared to say made a pleasanter noise than the rubber-core off any club, but I will admit that the new ball does make a very satisfactory one when struck by a driver. The big hitters make a much bigger noise than ordinary people. I know no more terrific crack than that of a perfectly struck drive by Mr. Wethered; it is like a pistol shot. It amuses me to harbour the belief that I could, with my eyes shut, tell the sound of his drive from anyone else's. Of course I could not, but I shall continue to say that I could. Similarly I feel as if I could tell by ear his sister's drive from that of all the other ladies.

These are the pleasant sounds of golf. There are others equally familiar but less pleasant. There is, for instance, the rattling and bumping of iron clubs one against the other as a small caddie who has been lingering behind tries to over-take his irate master. It is generally accompanied by loud hiccups—an affliction so common among caddies as to de-mand scientific research—and ends with a terrific crash as the luckless child trips over a hummock and falls prostrate. Then there is the sound of our foursome partner missing a crucial mashie shot by digging too deeply into the turf. The stroke sometimes known as a "grumph" makes a horrid, heavy, dead noise, quite unmistakable. We look in another direction, perhaps, in an agony of apprehension, as he plays his shot, and then "Hullo," we say, "I didn't like the sound of that one." Our ear has been all too true a monitor, for, sure enough, as we look round there is the ball climbing feebly into the air to fall into the cross-bunker over which it should have soared. A splash is, I suppose, only a splash, whether made by a golf ball or any other falling body; yet is there not something peculiarly and characteristically ominous about the splash of our own ball in a pond which we thought we had carried by the skin of our teeth? I feel almost inclined to say that the sound of splashing is quite different according as the water is casual or in a bunker, but that is to be too imaginative. Another watery sound that we know all too well in winter golf is the purring of the ball on a water-logged putting green. We have examined the green minutely in the hope of finding something that we could call a puddle, how-ever tiny, and so be able to lift. Honesty compels us to play the ball where it lies, and then—p-rrr! and the ball sends a small fountain spouting into the air and sits sulkily down after travelling exactly half way to the hole. When I think of that sound one particular and tragic scene comes before me. It is the third green at Worplesdon; the final of the Mixed Foursomes has come to the thirty-ninth hole in such a deluge of rain as I hope never to see again, and poor Miss Joy Winn and Mr. Longstaffe, who have fought so heroically, are trying in vain to force their ball with their putters over the sodden grass. Three times running they try, and still the ball is not in the hole. That was the cruellest ending to a good match that ever was seen and the wettest even at Worplesdon, where the pattering of rain on umbrellas, the swishing of macintoshes in the wind and the squelching of water in the shoes make inevitable music.

Finally, the custom of various eminent golfers of carrying a shooting stick and sitting down between strokes will soon add a new sound and a new terror to golf. I was playing with one of these illustrious heavyweights at Rye in January and our game was haunted by a peculiar eerie and melancholy piping. One of our four grew exceedingly restive under this affliction, but no culprit could be discovered; at length it was found to be the wind whistling through some joint of Mr.

John Morrison's shooting stick while he sat poised in placid majesty. I don't know whether this is a matter for a new rule or is only a question of etiquette.

MATCH MAKING

Match making at golf is one of the fine arts. Not perhaps in a mere single; in that case the argument is scarcely better than a greedy wrangle. It is otherwise in a foursome, when that which might be low and pettifogging seems somehow to take on a nobler quality; we haggle not for ourselves but for our side.

The machine-made golfer of the present day will hardly understand these remarks. He simply takes the handicaps of the four players, adds, subtracts, divides, and there is an end of the matter; but your true match maker of the ancient and traditional school spurns official handicaps. I have a friend who would amend Mr. Hardcastle in *She Stoops to Conquer*; he would say: "I love all things that are old—old wine, old friends, old books, and old golf." Even while I admire him, I sometimes find it difficult perfectly to reconcile his points of view. He has a zest for making a good match and he drives a hard bargain. At the same time he declares that niggling questions as to one stroke or two are beneath the notice of a Scottish golfer. Only the other day he was quoting to me with approval the words of that most charming and dignified old gentleman, Charlie Hunter, of Prestwick. When called upon to make a match, the sage would only admit three handicaps, four strokes, a third, and a half. If one side wanted more than a half, the disparity was too great and the match not worth the playing. If less than four strokes was in question, he would say: "I think you can play them," and the match was made on level terms.

There is much to be said for these views, and yet there have been moments when I have almost thought that my friend paid them only lip service. His method of procedure is familiar to all his admirers. On the way to the teeing ground he says to his partner: "You make the match. I leave all the arguing to you." He then withdraws himself ostentatiously to a few yards distance, "in search," as was said, I believe, of Lord Byron, "of the conspicuous solitude which that nobleman loved." The partner does his best; he tries all the usual moves; he flatters, he cajoles, he appeals for pity, and at long last a bargain is on the point of being struck. Then suddenly: "What's that, what's that?" cries my friend, who has apparently been examining the texture of a neighbouring green; he casts from him the mantle of aloofness and plunges into the fray. The whole question is re-opened, and the argument has even been known to continue over the matter of a single stroke after the first shots have been fired and while the combatants are walking along the causeway and over the pond.

A few days ago I took part in one of these scenes. My friend and I had yielded with ridiculous magnanimity on a point of two strokes, and we had had our reward. We had played level, and we had just won. Afterwards, in a moment of drowsy triumph, I picked up a book on golf published some time in the 'sixties, not so much a book as a pamphlet, written by some delightful and anonymous Scotsman who called himself "An old golfer" or "A keen hand". There I found something that came pat to my purpose, for it was an account of one of the very earliest competitions played under handicap. It took place on the Bruntsfield links. Not long before there had been played at St. Andrews a grand match-play tournament, in the nature of an unofficial Amateur Championship, in the final of which Mr. Robert Chambers, junior, had beaten the pawky Mr. Wallace, of Balgrummo. "The general rules of the Bruntsfield Tournament resembled those adopted at St. Andrews, but the mode of determining the rounds involved a very important difference. The Bruntsfield competition was settled by strokes, players being equalled by handicap."

Four rounds of the seven-hole course were played, and the competitors were divided into three classes, "the first class receiving no odds, the second class receiving twelve strokes, the third class receiving twenty strokes". This was carrying out Charlie Hunter's principle with a vengeance, since the difference between the first two classes was something more than a third. In the first class were some seven players, including the great Mr. Chambers, who was out of form. Mr. D. McCuaig, "graceful, scientific and certain", returned 151, and Mr. J. Williamson 154. The third class, the rabbits as we should call them in our vulgar modern tongue, did no manner of good, but in the second class there was a certain Mr. R. B. Shaw, whose score was "159, 12 off, 147". He seems to have been the object of envy, if not of suspicion. "Shaw," we are told, "played his very best game; indeed, so well that some were disposed to think that this competitor should have been placed in the first class."

I confess that my sympathies are warmly engaged on behalf of Mr. Shaw. For a player of his handicap he had done great deeds, and as this was a handicap competition, I cannot for the life of me see why he should not have won. This was not the opinion of the author of the book. "This is the point," he wrote, "which seems to us objectionable, that the first prize should be won by the adventitious aid of odd strokes. It cannot be doubted for a moment that the most beautiful display of golf craft was shown by James Williamson and McCuaig, and it was felt by every golfer that the palm had passed from deserving brows." That seems to me in the nature of a self-evident proposition, but it was the view of a famous golfer, the best amateur of his day, who disapproved of handicaps on the ground that they "obscured the issue". He may have been right and I shall certainly adopt his argument when next I prepare to tee my ball on the edge of the pond in a match against my old friend. It is my firm conviction that he will not see it. He will insist on the "adventitious aid" of all the strokes he can get out of me, and he will get at least two too many.

MORE STROKES, MORE FUN

The tearing up of a card is generally regarded as a rather discreditable business, showing at once vanity and pusillanimity in the tearer; and I must say that I do feel something more of a man when I have gone on to the bitter end and handed in the horrid thing. Circumstances, however, alter cases; there are occasions when, if only for the sake of the players behind, we are almost justified in the cowardly act, and I am about to write of one.

As a rule, when a golfer tears up a card he does so not merely figuratively, but literally, and no one but his marker knows the exact facts. A card has now come into my hands which, I think, its owner must have intended to destroy. He did not, however, and his marker first secreted it and then passed it on to another who, thinking that it might be useful, gave it to me. The whole business is, as you will perceive, a shady, if not a positively dishonourable, one. I feel rather ashamed of it; but so poignant a "human document" as this card cannot be allowed to lie hidden. So, with all due precautions of anonymity as to player and course, it shall be set out.

The score was compiled in a qualifying competition on a well-known seaside course, and here it is as far as it goes:

Out: 10, 12, 9, 9, 10, 7, 11, 9, 8.
Home: 12, 17, 12, 9, 20, 8.

That is to say, the player took 85 to go out and he had taken 78 for six holes on the way home when he gave up the unequal struggle. Statisticians will note that he took double figures at eight out of the fifteen holes played, and that his average score for a hole was 10 13-15. There appears to be some doubt whether the tally was duly kept. Both marker and player, though persons of the highest probity, may have grown a little tired, and one who played behind them declares that in the twenty recorded for the fourteenth hole "air shots were not counted". I entirely dissociate myself from any such slanderous statement, but there it is.

With nothing but the card and the length of the holes to help us, we must employ the methods of Sherlock Holmes if we are to discover anything about the round, and those methods, as Watson found, are easier to admire than to apply. We are probably justified in guessing that the wind rather favoured the player on the way out, but, on the other hand, his later falling off may only have been due to a natural and cumulative fatigue. In those first nine holes, I think, he must have played more or less his normal game, for there are no purple patches, and the two holes at which he took fewest strokes, the fifth and ninth, are both one-shot holes. He holed them in seven and eight respectively and, judged by that standard, his eleven at the seventh, which is 478 yards long, was a noteworthy achievement. On the way home, seventeen was superficially bad at the eleventh—a mere 352 yards long—but my recollection is that at this hole there is a deep and cavernous ditch running along the left of the fairway, and once the player is in it, anything might happen. Of course, the twenty at the fourteenth was a real tragedy, because this is only a one-shot hole of 162 yards. Heaven forbid that I should call it an easy three; it is not that, and especially not in a wind, but it is a little hard to understand where there is enough trouble to account for an "approximated" twenty.

No praise can be too high for the way in which, after this calamity, the player pulled himself together and did his second eight of the round, and that not this time at a one-shotter. This makes it all the sadder that he never holed out the sixteenth. It is a long and severe hole (510 yards) in hilly country, and I am told that the getting there was a long business. He had almost reached the green when suddenly his courage forsook him. His marker urged him to go on, but he answered quietly that he had "no chance *now*," and picked up his ball. So his card only remains a noble fragment. Had he been able to hole the last three holes in thirty-six shots—an average of twelve—he would just have beaten 200. There was a one-shotter coming at the seventeenth, where another eight might have been hoped for. Could he have done it? That we shall never know. An inscrutable riddle, he mocks us to the end of time.

It chanced that this card was handed to me at the hour of the cocktail in a place where people congregate before luncheon. Several sniggered over it with me, but there was one who took a rather different and more serious view. He said, possibly with some exaggeration, that his golf was of the same quality as that of the man who made the score, and that he and his like got much more pleasure out of the game than did superior persons. Would I, he asked, write an article to that effect, and then, in an inspired moment, he exclaimed: "More strokes, more fun, there's your title ready-made for you!" So, having adopted his suggestion, I must do the best I can with his subject, but I am not convinced that he is right. His title might be true of cricket, where, roughly speaking, the more strokes the more runs, or, at any rate, the more prolonged the innings. It might be moderately true of lawn tennis. Give me an opponent of exactly my own futile calibre, and we can now and again have quite a long rally by means of our mild little lobs backwards and forwards over the net, which we find exhilarating and enjoyable. Our strokes are contemptible, but they do, during that rally, attain two primary objects of getting the ball over the net and into the court. Our ambitions are strictly limited and are satisfied. On the other hand, the man who takes twelve to a hole at golf is nearly all the time failing miserably to attain his object: a large proportion of those twelve shots must be tops or fluffs, unless, indeed, they are, most of them, accounted for by a rapid rain of blows in a bunker which leave the ball *in statu quo*. And surely nobody, except a man who is blind with fury and wants to hit something, can enjoy mere unsuccessful thumping.

Admittedly, my friend, taking him at his own valuation, is much more easily pleased than the superior person. One good, honest drive, if he hits one, will give him a greater thrill than a champion will get from a whole round of perfectly struck tee shots. Just to see the ball rise into the air is, for him, something, and when it flies over a tall bunker and disappears into the happy valley beyond he is doubtless ecstatic. Moreover, he is not unduly bothered about hooks and slices; as long as the ball soars, its direction is a secondary consideration. Granted all these things, I still think that his joys are few. "I 'ate heights," said a famous professional, who did very few of them. The lowliest must come to hate them when they are part of the regular routine. If an eight could represent perfect play, judged even by the humblest standards, it would be a different matter, but on no course of my acquaintance is there a hole which can be described as "a good eight hole".

This is not to say that the very best of golfers must enjoy the game more than the next best, and so on down the scale. I do not believe that for a moment, but I do say that beyond a certain pitch of badness golf cannot be very much fun. Probably the exceedingly steady and trustworthy golfer with a handicap of five or six gets as much pleasure as most people. Within his powers he makes a great many good shots, he gets a little the best of it in match making, he wins, by means of his steadiness, a large proportion of matches and half-crowns. He is not tortured by mad ambitions to be a champion: but stay! is he not? We do not know what is going on inside that old grey head of his, and it may be that he would give all his steadiness just to hit one drive like that young slasher in front. "See how strangely we men are made!" said Prince Florizel.

A CHANCE FOR COLLECTORS

The postman has just brought me a document which is not, I trust, as pathetic as it appears. In any case, some little alteration of names and places is advisable in quoting it, since, as Dr. Watson once remarked: "It will be obvious that any details which would help the reader to exactly identify the criminal would be injudicious and offensive."

This document is headed "Notice to Golfers" and announces a fête for the church funds of, let us say, Puddlecombe. The date, on Watsonian principles, I suppress. "There will be on sale," it proceeds, "at attractive prices, a large number of golf clubs by celebrated makers, part of the well-known collection of Blank, Esquire." Next come the names of the famous artists who have fashioned the drivers, the brassies, the irons, and the putters. These are all set out in bold black type, and then follow, rather less conspicuously, these words: "All the above clubs, fitted with finest selected hickory shafts. Many of them new or little used." After the word "clubs" there is written in ink "63 in all" with two exclamation marks, and the handwriting, shaky with emotion, is undoubtedly that of Blank, Esquire, himself.

What can have caused the dispersal of this unique collection? Is it the hardness of the times which drives even the richest to such heartbreaking economies as carrying their own clubs or selling an old master? I do hope not, for I lunched admirably with Blank, Esquire, only the other day, and it would be dreadful to think that I had in effect been drinking his "Iron Clubs, rustless and otherwise, by Forgan, Auchterlonie, &c." Cleopatra and her pearl would be nothing to that. No, it cannot be, since in that case he would surely be keeping the profits for himself and not handing them over to the fête. Is it, then, a sign of the remorseless advance of steel? You observed, no doubt, those pregnant words "all fitted with

finest selected hickory shafts". Has Blank, Esquire, cast off
all his faithful old friends, some of them so new as not to be
old at all, at the caprice of this steel-hearted mistress? I know
he was coquetting with steel when last I played with him.
There was a clanking sound as his caddie toiled after him
with a full armoury; but this is worse than anything I could
have imagined.

There is a third and much less dismal possibility. It is simply
this, that Blank, Esquire, in the course of a spring-cleaning at
his house, discovered a cache of sixty-three clubs, the pos-
session of which he had totally forgotten, and said in an
expansive moment that Puddlecombe Church might as well
have them. This is on the whole the likeliest solution. It may
not appear so to ordinary people who acquire clubs on an
ordinary scale, but this man has been a Maecenas of the
club-makers. He buys clubs by the dozen and hides them by
fifties in a cave. There are racks of them in the passage
and bags of them among the coats and hats. As good an
approaching cleek as I ever had—I would not insult it by
calling it a jigger—I got from his pantry, not "at an attractive
price", but free, handed to me with the gesture of an Oriental
potentate who gives his guests any of his possessions that they
admire. Mr. Boffin loved to read about the hoards of misers,
how banknotes were found snug in the back of a drawer, or
tied up in an old jacket or in the chimney—"in nineteen
different holes, all well filled with soot". If Blank, Esquire's
house were ransacked, goodness only knows where clubs
would not be found.

He has the soul of an artist and loves a beautiful club for
its own sake. He is also, as are most of us, always on the
verge of discovering the great secret. When a new driver seems
to have brought him for the moment nearer to his goal, he is
gripped at the heart by a chill fear lest something should
happen to that driver, and instantly orders five more like it.
Then he finds that there is a subtle lack of harmony between
that driver on the one side and his brassy and his graduated
spoons on the other. So the brassy and the spoons retire to
the pantry to make room for a new and usurping clan. A little
later a fresh spoon seems to have possessed a certain *je ne sais
quoi* suggestive of higher things, and so, beginning at the

opposite end of the scale, a similar process of discarding and refilling takes place. If the same sort of thing happens only two or three times a year in the case of a "harmonised" or "Co-ordinated" set of irons, it will be understood how quickly and almost imperceptibly a house can silt up with clubs.

I have not been entirely honest about this sale. I have kept to myself one item calculated to make a collector's mouth water. I did so in the hopes of being able to attend the fête myself, but my conscience reproaches me, and, besides, I should never be able to afford it. Therefore, I will reveal the fact that among the sixty-three are some "St. Andrews Wooden Putters". Moreover, these were no putters ignorantly bought off the peg; these were lovingly and leisurely fashioned to order, as the notice states "by Jamies Anderson". If the golfers of that most charming course at Puddlecombe are half the men I take them for, they will make a rush for these treasures, and the funds of the fête will go up by great bounds. In that case, it would be no more than right that there should be a little stained-glass window in Puddlecombe Church, depicting Blank, Esquire, after the manner of St. Andrew, with his cross of two wooden putters. In point of fact, he uses an aluminium one nowadays, but nobody need know that.

A PLAYER'S DESTINY

A German artist called Otto Nückel has drawn a novel called *Destiny*. He tells his story in no words but in a series of woodcuts so forcible and fierce and terrifying that they make your flesh creep.

You follow the heroine from the cradle to the grave, and save for the clue given by the title to each series of pictures you must ferret out the story for yourself. Her drunken father is run over by a tramcar, her mother sets alight to herself by upsetting a lamp. Then, when she is leading a comparatively happy pastoral life, and leading a goat in from its pasture by the light of the setting sun, there arrives the seducer, a too plausible commercial traveller. There follows a long string of episodes, all in the end tragical; the good plumber who rescues her from a life of infamy; the prosperous tailor who marries her, in his dress clothes, with an iron cross on his breast; the sinister hunchback who dogs her steps; the detectives who pursue her with bloodhounds, fat men but of a macabre fatness, as plump and as frightening as Count Fosco himself. I cannot recount it all. Enough that in the end she piles all her furniture against the door in an agony of terror, that the door is burst down and that she leaps to her death out of the window, pursued by flashing revolver shots from the fat detectives.

Even as I shivered with horror over these astonishing pictures, my warped and one-sided mind was translating them into terms of golf. Here was the ideal way in which to present the golfer's miserable life. It has its glad moments; Mr. Nückel's heroine had those, as when she went to a circus or a jollification in a café, or lay dreaming in a boat under the moon in the arms of the virtuous plumber; but taken as a whole the golfer's life is tragic. At any rate, it was thus I drew my hero's life as I sat seeing woodcuts in the fire; and here briefly is how it runs.

The first series of pictures, by comparison cheerful, is called, I think "The First Club". He goes with his father to a golf course, a muddy common intersected by ditches, with a factory chimney standing out against a lurid sky. Fascinated by the game, he is given a small club; you see him swinging it vigorously in the garden at home, but observe already that the seeds of tragedy are sown—he is overswinging himself, his infantile right knee is too flexible and his right elbow too high in the air. Presently he is taken for a summer holiday to a seaside course. Here there is a Martello tower, which looks extremely effective in a woodcut, black with a sunset behind it. The boy plays by himself, dodging illicitly among the grown-ups; once he does the second hole in three, and once, supreme moment of bliss, he carries the bunker at the last hole. Tragedy is in wait, however. He has a lesson from the professional, who points at his right knee; that *must* be kept stiffer; the reckless child does not care, for he has just carried the bunker, but you, the reader, can see that he is doomed. Worse still, he gets extremely cross; he throws his clubs about when he misses a shot. He is reproved for doing so and promises amendment; he looks rather a pitiful little figure, also against the setting sun, as he walks penitently home along the top of the cliff; but you know that he will continue to get cross for all the rest of his life and will want to break clubs over his knee.

The next few years of the hero's life are passed rapidly over. You find him now almost grown-up. He has done a quite absurdly good score and beaten bogey by several holes; the handicapping committee are seen sitting over his card in solemn conclave, and reduce him to scratch. He is insufferably pleased with himself, when immediately afterwards he becomes an undergraduate and goes back to play on that same muddy common where he had his original little club. And now you come to a really ghastly series of pictures entitled "The Slice". Suddenly his ball begins to fly far to the right; you see it a white speck curving horribly against an angry cloud. It is retrieved from ditches by lurking ruffians, having about them something indescribably evil, like the fat detectives. He goes home and flings himself on his bed in an agony of remorse. Why, why had not he listened years ago to what the professional said about his right knee? There comes a little relief to the gloom. You turn the page to a scene of wild hilarity. Tiny figures in dress clothes are dancing ecstatically by the banks of a muddy stream, with an old town seen by moonlight in the background. Being supernaturally astute, you guess that this is Sandwich; that Oxford has been beaten and that the hero has won his match. So he has, but look again at the picture and you will discern in the densest of the shadow an ominous and crouching figure, like Mr. Nückel's hunchback. You don't know who it is, and no more do I precisely, but there is something fatal about it; it means that the poor hero will slice again very soon, that he will be a hopeless, haunted man for ever and ever.

I said that the adventures of Mr. Nückel's heroine were too long to recount, and now I find that my hero's are even longer. I must skip over many years with their petty successes and failures; he wins a medal or two, plays a match or two, and—you observe his essentially contemptible nature—is rather good at beating ladies. Then you see gradually his decline and fall. His putting entirely leaves him, no doubt because in the first series (I forgot to mention that picture) he would learn to putt with a mashie. There is one brief interlude of cheerfulness when he gets a steel-shafted club. Once again by the rays of the setting sun, you see him practising with it; a little stiffly but still joyfully he dances after the ball; he thinks he has got it all back. Turn over to the next page and there is the handicap committee sitting again, cruel-looking men with bald, shiny heads. You know exactly what they are saying: "Poor old chap, he really is no good now; we must put him up." The sun goes down for the last time. One by one in the gathering dusk the hero takes out his clubs and gives them a farewell waggle. Then he puts his head in the oven and turns on the gas.

A CHRISTMAS ANTIDOTE

Christmas comes but once a year. Mr. Thomas Tusser is believed to have been the first man who made that statement, and it is tolerably certain that he never made a more comforting one.

It is a very good day in its way, but presumably no one will deny that most people eat too much on it, and have too little to do. There are, I am aware, wretches who with a flagrant cynicism, leave their homes and go elsewhere to play golf, but they are outside the pale; I am thinking of reasonably domestic and virtuous persons. For them, or let me boldly say for us, it would be all very well if we could, as did the Dingley Dellers, take "a five-and-twenty mile walk to get rid of the effects of the wine at breakfast". That happened, to be exact, on the 23rd, and not the 25th, assuming it to have happened at all, but of course, it never did; it is a glorious and fantastic fiction, and what the party really did was to sleep soundly at Manor Farm throughout the afternoon. That is too often what we do, and it produces a Scrooge-like demeanour on recovering consciousness. To avoid this, I have even slunk away to putt at table-legs, but few are capable of such heroic folly, and the results, golfing or otherwise, are not satisfactory. There must be something better to do, and I believe I have found it.

It was partly the fog last week that did it, partly the memory of a kind friend in Ireland with whom I sometimes stay. The fog was so thick that even the mildest little shots vanished from sight. It was dull and rather eerie work, to pace up and down a lonely valley through a blanket of wet white mist in search of a mud-blackened ball. Then I remembered my Irish friend, who used every evening to hit full drives backwards and forwards across his lawn with a kind of soft ball. I set out on my quest, and returned with a box of them, masquerading as real golf balls in paper wrappings. Perhaps this magic ball should not strictly be called soft. It is superficially hard; it is rather larger than a golf ball, and appears to be dressed in flannel. Possibly it is made of cork or something of that sort. I do not know, and having, thank goodness, an unscientific mind, I have not the faintest wish to dissect it and find out. This, at any rate, is what it does: it flies off the club with the speed of thought, then soars in a graceful arc and falls limply to the ground at a distance of some fifty yards. My Irishman, who is a person of vast golfing erudition, did the thing in the highest style. He ruled a straight line by means of a piece of string pegged down at either end. In the middle of that line he teed his ball, and thus endeavoured to observe whether he was swinging "from inside out". I cannot live up to his standard, but I have at least grown agreeably warm and have formed several agreeable theories without having to leave the garden.

Whatever else this ball may be, it is no flatterer. It exposes the player's frailties with utter ruthlessness. I read lately an instructive remark of Henry Cotton's about the larger and lighter ball which becomes the official American ball on New Year's Day; he said that it "required a more varied and more highly perfected technique." These are formidable expressions, but they are inadequate to describe this ball of mine. I knew my technique was imperfect, but I never knew how imperfect till I tried my first few strokes. The shot, as we say when we want an excuse, felt all right, but the result was certainly all wrong, for the ball flew away to the off side in a most malignant curve, and lodged in a fir tree, whence it had to be dislodged with sticks. The slightest tendency to cut seemed to be so horribly exaggerated that in my vanity I exclaimed against the ball, but it was not the ball's fault, for a severe course of anti-slicing treatment ultimately made it fly like an arrow from the bow. There is, I think, some knack in driving it which is not so necessary with a real golf ball, but it is a wholly virtuous knack, since it seems to consist chiefly in smoothness of hitting, and that never did anybody any harm. After a series of rather sparkling drives with it, it was impossible to resist a move from the lawn to the field for some strokes with a real ball. It would have been shattering to a new-found faith if these had been unsuccessful, but they were, on the contrary, exceedingly gratifying.

Now to return to my text of Christmas, here is not merely an antidote, but a pleasant resource for that trying day. There will be no more sleeping or sulking, no more boredom in having to look at other people's presents, no more conscious-ness of guilt in not being grateful enough for our own. At the very first tendency towards any of these sensations, out will come those dear little balls from their box, and they will be battered to and fro till a positive yearning for more plum pudding makes itself felt. Nay, more, I will not selfishly confine these benefits to myself, I will drag the whole household out into the garden and given them catches with my driver. It will be just what they want to brace them up.

ARCTIC JOYS

"All things," said Prince Florizel, "come to an end, the evil like the good, pestilence as well as beautiful music." So it is even possible that some day this wind will stop blowing from the north-east; but at the moment when I sit down by the fire, clasping an icy pen in be-mittened fingers, what is there to think or write about but the weather?

Even if the subject were not so compelling it would, I confess, tempt me in order that I might give the puff oblique to a little heroism of my own. Let it be said to the credit of the general sanity that it is not everybody who would have played four rounds of golf at the last week-end, and that on one of the least sheltered courses in the Kingdom, where the wind is popularly believed to come, unstymied, from the Steppes of Russia. Still rarer is the man who at the end of the two days could have laid his hand on his heart and said that he had thoroughly enjoyed them. That is my case, at once ridiculous and sublime. Nor was I alone, for on the Saturday evening, when the battle was over, sixteen persons sallied out again to play a one-club match in the gathering dusk. Even as there is magic and madness in a midsummer night, so there must be something of it, I think, in a mid-winter day. Or was it only that we were at enchanted Worlington?

I do not wish to pose, and there were times when I wished myself well out of it. Duty had been done on the Saturday, and Sunday was to have been a day of watching in many greatcoats, but an invitation to play against Cambridge as a substitute for that illustrious society called the Moles was too much for my vanity, and I gave in. Next morning there seemed a horrid irony in the title of our side. How pleasant to have been a real mole, a "little gentleman in black velvet", who lived snug underground in his own dug-out. It was pleasant enough snug in a car looking out at the blue sky and the sun, and trying not to see the trees quivering in the wind. If only, I thought, that warm, cosy journey could go on for ever; but the miles grew fewer and fewer, all too soon we were there, and a partner was waiting with some impatience on the first tee.

There is one thing essential on these occasions, and that is not to fall into the vulgar error of not putting on enough clothes. Mittens for the hands and a scarf for the neck are obvious precautions, and policeman's macintosh trousers help to retain some vestige of sensation in the legs. The real problem lies in the number of waistcoats, woolly or otherwise, that can be crowded on under the coat or leather jerkin. For myself, I was conscious of resembling one of the players in the Dingley Dell cricket match, the "very stout gentleman, whose body and legs looked like half a gigantic roll of flannel elevated on a couple of inflated pillow-cases". The club felt as if it would never get up; when it had traversed half its course there seemed to come a general cracking and sticking, and the "follow through" was but a courtesy title. Still, the ball generally rose into the air and ended after a short but scrupulously straight flight upon grass, and I did keep warm. Yes, I will say that again and let my traducers, as Mr. Pott remarked, "writhe in impotent malice"; *I did keep warm.*

It is impossible on such a day to aim at too high a standard in the matter of clothing. It is very necessary, for the ordinary golfer at any rate, not to aim at too high a standard in the matter of play. If he does, he will be inevitably disappointed, and will play all the worse for it. There is no particular reason for missing tee shots, but a proportion of misses in all the other shots had better be boldly faced. Brassy shots are the hardest of all, especially when the ball lies close, for the colder we are the more we top, and the more we try to avoid topping the more we dig. A spoon on the course is worth two brassies in the bush, and it is a great mistake to play too proud a game. Iron play is difficult, of course, but by no means impossible; it is when we get to the putting that it is so important not to expect too much of ourselves or our partner. Given rather bare greens, some of them of puzzling slopes, and all of a deliciously "kittle" character, with an icy wind sweeping across them, there is no man alive who can be sure of laying even a reasonably long putt dead, or of holing one when he is dead. In the long putts the ball creeps and crawls until it has almost reached the hole, then out of sheer devilry puts on a little spurt and runs just those deadly four feet past. In the short ones it sidles and wriggles like an eel; it either takes a borrow which Sherlock Holmes could not see if he lay flat on his stomach with a microscope, or else refuses to take one which even Lestrade or Gregson could see with the naked eye. If in these circumstances we grow quickly dissatisfied we shall miss everything, and be exceedingly un-pleasant to play with into the bargain. Far better to plume ourselves absurdly on the smallest achievement, for then the Fates will now and again relent and reward us with a glorious accident.

The evening one-club match, with four players a-side and each club played strictly in turn, is a great feature of Worlington, and on the first evening, as I said, this fine tradition was finely maintained. The orthodox match is over a three-hole course from the first tee to the second hole, third tee to the fourth hole, from the fifth tee over the fir trees and so home to the ninth hole. The stakes consist as a rule of so much a stroke, and there are places on the course where a prolonged stay can be very expensive. To see the other party in a thorn bush, iron following driver, mashie following iron, then putter, then driver again with the ball still unmoved—this is to taste not perhaps one of the most exalted, but certainly one of the most satisfying, of human joys.

Nothing so poignant happened this time, but one side did suffer from a permanent grievance. After some skilful manoeuvring for position, short here and round there, we foresaw a clear gain of two strokes as we came to that fatal hogs-backy second green. The enemy had to take a wooden club for an impossible short pitch from the left over two hazards. Our wooden club player—he had a spoon more-over—was perfectly situated in front of the green with a simple run-up of thirty yards or so to play. As we all told him, a spoon was the very club of all clubs we should have chosen for the shot. He might have laid it dead, he must have putt it quite close to the hole. In fact, he nearly missed the globe and only reached the abject suburbs of the green. From that blow we never recovered; the side was divided against itself, and as each man came in to the club-house and was asked how he had fared, he began: "We were doing splendidly until that fellow B with his spoon—"

However, it was all such fun, on such a noble course, so full of a fine Pickwickian atmosphere of roaring fires and cherry brandy, that even B was forgiven in time, and personally I shall make a point of never alluding to the circumstance again.

AFTER TEA

About the beginning of March—it was this time on the first of the month—there is played each year at Worlington the match between Cambridge and their elders of the Society. On the following day the men of Worlington, sometimes with one or two undergraduate reinforcements, knock out of the Society any conceit of themselves that they may have acquired on the day before.

The thought of these two matches brings back all manner of pleasant memories, but there is one in particular which cannot possibly belong to any other time or place. When the Saturday's match is over and the tea and sponge cake, that must have been made by fairy fingers, there takes place a game which is something much more than that—it is a sacred and traditional rite. Two teams sally out, each under a proved leader; they consist of five players apiece, each of the five is armed with one club, and they have got to play a strict rotation, each with his own club, "thorough bush, thorough brier", sometimes putting with a driver, sometimes playing heavily cut pitches with an aluminium putter. It is a noble game, but it has been described before, and I will not dwell on its niceties. In this instance, however, it has a symbolic meaning. To the visitors at any rate, it stands for the first round after tea, and if it is still played centuries hence, as I hope it will be, anthropologists of that era will write books to prove that it was by this religious ceremonial that primitive peoples celebrated the return of spring.

There are some pleasures in life that we are inclined to disparage when we can no longer feel quite such a zest for them as of old, but the first round or two after tea are not among these. He would be a curmudgeon indeed who did not enjoy them, if only vicariously. We did not all go out to take part in that Worlington rite; some of us only watched the first tee shots from the veranda, and then set out for Cambridge; but as we disappeared, like Hiawatha, "in the glory of the sunset", and as we drove soberly home down Bottisham Hill and past Quy Church, we liked to think of those young heroes playing yet one more hole and then still another in the dusk among the firs.

There is that about golf after tea, even if we do not play a game, but only chip about with a mashie, which is of a scrumptious and heavenly quality—so heavenly indeed that, whether or not it is very selfish of me, I like to play it best by myself. In fact, I have just come this moment from doing so. There was something consciously surreptitious in the way in which I crept noiselessly out of the house and so into the field. There was no earthly reason for this parade of secrecy, no callers in the drawing-room who might see me through the window; but it added to my enjoyment to play at this Red Indian game and to take infinite care lest my two new steel shafts should betray me by clanking against one another. Besides, I had the field to myself. There is a horse that lives in this field. He is a thoroughly amiable horse, but of rather too friendly and inquisitive a nature. I do not think he takes any particular interest in golf, but he is a born spectator, and comes prancing at me so sociably as to disturb the perfect concentration. On this blessed occasion he had been put to bed early; I caught a glimpse of him looking wistfully out of his stall, I knew that all was well and so to slogging.

That last is not a good golfing word, but it is used deliberately. There is a delicious temptation to hit hard after tea, because at that time the stiffest of us feel comparatively lithe and lissom. It seems easier to cultivate that beautiful, impalpable little pause at the top of the swing, to wait and gather ourselves together and bang the ball with an internal cry of: "This shall not go for naething." To-morrow morning we shall be as stiff as ever again and stiffer, the gift of timing will have gone as utterly as has the sunset, but after tea we can still have our "moments of glad grace". Whether the ball really goes farther than it does earlier in the day I am not prepared to say on oath. At any rate we think it does, and that, when we are by ourselves, is all that matters. The enchantment of the hour lends distance to the shot, and the darker it gets the farther the ball appears to go. It is a mistake to become so enthusiastic as to measure the shot, for that, step we never so short, is a disillusioning process. In this field I know my distances pretty well, but I never let myself remember them after tea; and so home, flushed, elated, "and in my heart some late lark singing"; my goodness! how those shots did go.

I once saw the spring come in a land of storks. The sun was growing stronger and the light drawing out, and every day we looked anxiously for the storks to come to their old nests in the village of mud houses that lay across the river bed. At last they came, and one fine morning there they were— standing on one leg in the sunshine with a balance that roused a hopeless envy in the golfing heart. And then that night there came softly a big silent fall of snow, and next day the poor storks were clearly remarking that they had rejoiced too soon. I am going to play seaside golf this week-end, and it may be with me as it was with the storks, but nothing can rob me of what has been. Once again I have played after tea.

AQUATICS

"From an artistic point of view," said the retired headmaster, looking out over the waste of waters, "it will be a pity when it goes away."

We were standing on the club-house veranda with water lapping round our toes and the scene was undoubtedly pretty. A great lagoon stretched away to the mountain which guards the third green, broken only by a few islets of turf. The sun was sinking, not a breath of wind ruffled the surface, and the long row of sandhills were reflected in the placid depths. Yes, it was beautiful, and it was all very well for a retired headmaster to say so, for his life, save for a mild flirtation with school inspecting, is one long holiday, and he could wait tranquilly till the floods receded; but we had only a bare week in which to amuse ourselves. He is a kindly, broad-minded man and he saw our point of view. "You'll find it better," he said, "once you get past the third. If you miss out the tenth and eleventh, I think you can cross by the Causeway—it ought to be clear now—and play the twelfth. There's really no reason why you should lose a ball." So out we went.

In his generous desire to please, I cannot help thinking that he had somewhat overstepped the truth, for when we got back to the club-house after our first round and took stock of our joint resources we found that we had lost between us a matter of seven balls. Some of them were really lost. One honest slice or hook and they plunged to their doom. We could only stand on the brink and say that somewhere deep down in those "black and dowie waters" lay the beautiful ball which only a few minutes before had been full of life, fresh from its paper. There was sadness in the thought but by comparison little bitterness; the water gods had loved that ball and it had died young. It was otherwise with the ball which had only run gently down a slope into the lake. We could see it shining where it lay, but it was always just too far off for us to reach it. We might possibly tie two clubs together with a handkerchief and fish for it, but then if the knot gave way, as it probably would, we should lose a club as well as a ball. Or we might take off our shoes and stockings, and to paddle would be "an awfully big adventure", but it would also be a chilly and cheerless start to a round. We decided to leave the ball there and perhaps when we came back we could borrow a net. Alas! When we did come back we scanned the waters in vain; some amphibious gentleman in sea-boots had been there in our absence and reaped a rich harvest.

In our succeeding rounds we did not lose nearly so many balls, for we had learnt wisdom. We came reluctantly to the conclusion that we had better not play the temporary first and second holes which some kind person had laid out for us. They had their points, but as the fairways were all of blown sand and the greens were rather like bunkers and the floods engulfed any ball that was ten yards off the line, there was at least something to be said against them. So we began at the third, where there is a great deal of sand but no water, and after that it was "all wery capital". If we got into bunkers, of course we had to lift and lose a stroke, and the greens were rather oozy, and the ball showed a tendency to screw back after pitching, and now and again you might get a little mud in your eye; but still all things are comparative; the sun was shining on the sea and the bracken on the hills looked lovely. We even grew so brave that one day we thought of playing the tenth and eleventh holes. "What do you think?" we asked our one caddie. "Could we do it?" "Well, sir," he replied, looking at the least futile driver of the three of us, "you *might*." A resolution that the holes be not played was carried by two votes to one.

From any set of golfing circumstances there are lessons to be learnt, and golf on a flooded course ought to teach something about keeping the eye on the ball. This is a very difficult thing to do on turf that is sodden with water, and yet if you try really hard to do it the results are appalling, for to get down to the ball too much is far worse than not to get down to it at all. Fling the head up in the air and half top it and at least you may hope to compass a certain distance by the duck and drake stroke. Try to look like J. H. Taylor in a picture book and a moist and ignoble fluff will probably ensue.

Let it not be thought that I write in a bitter spirit. Far from it: there was much to be thankful for. "Think how much better this is than staying indoors," one of our party constantly remarked after hitting his ball off the extreme nose of his driver in the direction of silly point, into a deep rushy pool over the railway line. It was—much better; and never did tea taste so nearly divine as after two rounds of our aquatic game. Again we were always hoping; each morning the high-water mark on the edge of the lagoon showed that the floods had gone down to the extent of at least one inch. And finally do not let me forget all the drain shop that was talked. It was, I admit, a little over my head, but still it sounded very interesting. There were some drains, it appeared, which grew narrower and narrower as they got nearer to the sea—that struck me as odd—and there was one which was a kind of Mrs. Harris, since there was considerable reason to believe that there was no such a drain. There was another—the most important, the most feverishly discussed drain of all—as to which the chief drain expert had come to this conclusion, that there was nothing for it but a charge of dynamite. Night and morning I listened for the roar that should proclaim its fate. I feel that on all accounts that is the way to deal with it.

AN EXTINCT CRATER

If you consult a doctor it is, on the whole, the wisest thing to do what he tells you. If, when you get home, you think that you know a pill worth two of his, that his views on smoking are clearly absurd, and that he would have said something quite different if he had as long an experience of your constitution as you have yourself, you might just as well have saved your guineas.

These platitudes have a golfing application. Experts are often called in to doctor golf courses. They prescribe the changing of tees, the digging of bunkers, and so forth, and they are listened to with an outward show of respect. When they have gone away the local wiseacres begin to discuss the matter. They say that the great man would never have made such ludicrous suggestions if he had known the course in summer (or winter), in an east (or west) wind; they condemn certain of his bunkers because their own best shots always finish in those particular places, and so, in the end, his prescription is whittled away to nothing. On the beloved course where I have been playing—or, to be more exact, perhaps, paddling—during this week, I have, in the course of years, twice seen this whittling process carried out. Two highly distinguished architects have at different times come to advise us, and the only traces of their visits consist in one solitary bunker and the approaching of a certain green from a different angle than of old. If they were to come and see the course to-day they would probably make much the same comment as the charity boy did when he got to the end of the alphabet.

That, however, is not the end of the story, because now a third expert has been called in; he has spotted the links with pegs denoting new bunkers, and every single one of those bunkers is really going to be made. It is wonderful, but it is true. Already a new tee is springing up in one place and a new

green in another, and when, having putted grossly short, I
call Heaven to witness that the green has not been cut, my
friends try to soothe my anguish by telling me that all hands
are engaged upon the alterations. Everybody, I suppose, thinks
this, that, and the other, but nobody says anything, and
through this blessed outbreak of common sense I have no
doubt that the course will be greatly improved.

Having said so much, I must have my one little lament. I
have a profound respect for all architects, and I am sure this
one is as wise as an owl; I am not ill-disciplined, I am only a
little sad. The Crater green is going to disappear, nay, has
actually disappeared already. I hereby say publicly that the
new hole will be better than the old one ever was, and now,
like Mr. Pecksniff, "having discharged—I hope with tolerable
firmness—the duty which I owed to society, I will retire to
shed a few tears in the back-garden, as a humble individual."

Let me throw off all disguise and say that this hole is the
fifteenth at Aberdovey. It has been there and has been called
the Crater for hard on forty years. Originally it was a perfect
crater with a bank all round it. You could either pitch or
scuffle the ball into it, and if you hit hard enough, and the
hole was cut at the farther end of the green, there was more
than a reasonable chance that the ball, after making a circular
tour, would lie stone dead off the back wall. The first attempt
at reform was made by some strait-laced persons who disapproved of the scuffling shot. They planted the bank in front
of the green with tufts of bent grass which came to be known
by the irreverent name of "the pineapples". At first they were
thick and strong and resisted the running ball stoutly enough,
so that the second shot had perforce to be played in the air,
but the niblick gradually did its deadly, hacking work, and it
became possible to scuffle once more. This happened so long
ago that to say that you remember the pineapples is now
tantamount to admitting that you have one foot in the grave.

Some time later there came another reform; the bank in
front and some part of the banks on either side were cut away,
but that at the back remained. The green was no longer a
crater, but it retained its name and some at least of its
characteristics. To get on to the green was not so infallibly to
stay on it as in old days, but Fortune did give you a pleasant

kick now and then, and there was always a hope of a three. Incidentally, the tee was put back, and two such good shots were needed to reach the green at all that the three, when it came, had not been ill earned.

And now that long chapter in the hole's history is definitely over. What was left of the crater has already been filled up, and there is to be a long, narrow green, rising gently to a plateau at the far end. It will, I take it, be something after the style of the new "Lake" green at Hoylake, which has also replaced an old and circular friend. It will be guarded, as was its predecessor, on either side—on the right by broken, benty, sandy ground, and on the left by the road of cavernous ruts and the railway line. It will be, especially in a cross wind, a magnificent hole, but it will not be the Crater. That name I will never utter again. It ought to be kept sacred, as were the names of dead kings among the Kukuanas (see *King Solomon's Mines* passim), only to be spoken under penalty of instant death.

There! I have said my say and will now dry my tears. Perhaps there is some excuse for inflicting the story of the Crater on those who have never seen that vanished green, because the question of the retaining or abolishing holes of this sort is always arising. There are really two questions. The first is whether a hole that has existed for a long time and has been affectionately regarded does or does not earn a prescriptive right to remain as it was. The second is whether an intrinsically bad hole is not sometimes better than an orthodox one, if it be amusing and unlike all the others on the course. I will not attempt to answer either of them, and, indeed, I feel that despite my protestations I have been rather ill-disciplined after all. Poor, dear old Crater! Lightly lie the plateau's turf upon thee!

OUT OF THE WINDOW

On this day, that is to say on December 27th, which, as I write, is only creeping towards me with leaden feet, I shall be, if all is well, in a train. My clubs will be in the rack over my head, so that I can look at them now and then to reassure myself that they are there, and the journey will be pleasantly long enough to give me plenty of time for anticipation. I am thinking about it so much that golf out of a train window seems the only possible theme.

It is not a wholly unfruitful one, for it can take several forms. There are, for instance, those delicious moments in which the train draws near to the course on which we are going to play. It is good to come through Troon and Monkton to Prestwick with the noble line of sandhills stretching away on the right and, as we begin to slow down, the first green and the Alps and, if we are lucky, a friend greeting us with a slice out of bounds from the first tee. Sandwich has its moment, too, if we come to it from the side of Deal and can see the Maiden in the distance; and of course St. Andrews is best of all, for the excitement rises gradually to a climax. First we see the Eden and put our noses out to snuff the salt breeze; next the Eden course, then the Elysian Fields, and then the Corner of the Dyke.

It is another and quite different sensation to catch sight of courses that we know as we speed past them in an express. Every golfer has his own particular and familiar glimpses. When I go from Euston I look out for the third hole at Oxhey; on the way from King's Cross to Cambridge there is an affectionate glance to be cast at Royston heath; and from Paddington I never let myself grow too much immersed in my paper till I have seen the now be-bungalowed muddiness that was once West Drayton, and have wondered why in the world anybody ever played there. The journey from Waterloo affords, of course, the richest feast, beginning with the pleasant little Common at Esher, that used to be dotted with red coats, through Byfleet and Woking and West Hill and Bramshot. There must be some who came home from the War by Southampton and still recall the unspeakable thrill of seeing that those lovely courses were still there. Yes, there was the short seventh at Woking still sidling its way along the line. And the fifth green bowered in trees and best of all that little beast of a Principal's Nose in the middle of the fourth fairway, ready to trap the free and demobilised tee shot.

That was a special occasion when the mere sight of the course was more than enough; but in the ordinary way we always hope that we shall see somebody playing a stroke, by preference a bad one, that we can jeer at him without our ill-breeding being discovered. There is, however, some perverse chance in the matter which always makes us just too early or too late, as there is, by the way, in cricket out of a window, wherein a wicket has always just fallen as we come by. Either the players are walking after the ball or else one of them is indulging in a waggle so prolonged and ornate that we are whirled away craning our necks before he comes to the point. Sometimes they deliberately stop until we have passed, from some nonsensical fear that the rush and the roar of us should distract their attention. It is a thoroughly unsportsmanlike and dog-in-the-manger line of conduct, for they know perfectly well that we long to see a good foozle. They ought to rejoice in our puffing and snorting, as giving them an opportunity for practising concentration of mind.

This journey of mine, to which I am so looking forward, will take some six hours, but it will be very poor in golf courses. I can only think of one jolly little short hole that I shall see, down a steep hill to a pretty green ringed round with bunkers. That will be quite close to London, and after that I shall gaze in vain. The train will go through some almost romantically ugly black country, where there perhaps will be boys playing football on slag heaps, but there will be no golf courses. That is sad, because there ought to be such unpleasant ones, smoky and grimy and oozy, where the ball is constantly getting black. I should enjoy that, because it would give an added poignancy to my expectations. I should like to lean out and shout: "Ha, ha! you poor wretches. I'm going to the sea and to sandhills and bents. Don't you wish you were me?" However, the mind, if I may so term it, which is addled by golf has its compensations, and even when there are no courses, the traveller can see holes in every field, and "hooks in the running brooks", or, in my own case, probably slices. He can, in imagination, drive diagonally across that meadow to where the red cow is grazing, and then there is just time before the train has sped on for a "dog-leg" turn and a pitch over the hedge to a green by the oak tree; I can see even now one or two places on the way where I have before laid out these imaginary holes. There is one when I shall be drawing near to my journey's end. There is a little lonely chapel with "Bethel" written on it, and a valley with some bracken and a cheerful hill stream. I cannot now remember precisely how the hole goes, but it will come back to me when the time comes, and a little farther on there will come on the other side of the line a river that has such serpentine bends that one could carry it twice with a single shot, as one can the Barry Burn at Carnoustie. There is a good dream hole to be laid out there, but by that time I shall be almost too much excited to think it out. Finally, at the last stop of all there will be some of the most perfect turf in the world, kept daily fresh and beautiful by the tide, but, alas! darkness will have fallen and there will be nothing to see, unless, indeed, a welcoming moon be shining for me on the pools.

Meanwhile, I had better go and relieve my feelings by prematurely packing my clubs, with a large umbrella and my thickest boots in case of floods. I have been wondering whether, this year, I should take a shooting stick. The truly great always go round with shooting sticks nowadays, but I think I am like Uriah Heep, too humble, and had better not offend my betters by imitating them.

HEROISM IN THE RAIN

I wonder what it is that on a bright, sunshiny morning sets me musing, almost with affection, on golf in the rain. It is, I fancy, because I have been thinking about a place to which I am bound, where in long past Augusts I seem to have been more constantly and heroically wet than anywhere else in the world. I must not say where it is, lest the local lodging-house keepers have the law on me, but perhaps there may be one or two who can read between the lines.

Whenever I recall it there comes in my ears a gentle, steady sound of pattering. I had heard it dimly during the night on the roof of the old out-house where I slept in company with a vast and ancient duck-gun. Now, here in the morning, when I was broad awake and thinking about my train and my round, it was still relentless. Rain pattering on the beech tree and dripping down on to the slate steps underneath it, rain on the veranda, rain crowning the top of the hill behind the house with a misty halo, rain everywhere except under the big yew that could resist any downpour, so that there was a dry playground beneath its branches and one could go there to swing a despairing club. There was always the hope that, though it was wet in the hills, it might be fine by the seashore. Such things had been and might be again. So there came the bicycle ride to the station, splashing through puddles, and the stamping up and down the platform to dry wet legs, and the dreary wait for the train that was half an hour late. And sometimes when the train got to the junction there were signs of clearing, and when it got to the links the rain had stopped. And sometimes—much more often—it had not and did not intend to, and till lunch-time one read the illustrated papers of three months before, and after lunch one went out to face it.

There are some courses where the adventurer can say to his

partner that if it is too bad when they get to the third hole
they can give it up—that, at any rate, they can stop at the turn.
We were not so pampered; the course ran straight out and
home again, and there could be no returning save by the
longest and most dismal of walks; to start was to go through
with it. Moreover, at that time James Braid had not set the
fashion of wearing policeman's waterproof trousers, which
has doubtless saved many lives. It was a case of soggy flannels
that wreathed themselves round the legs, or knickerbockers,
the knees of which came to feel like twin lakes. How our shoes
did squelch, especially if we sliced into the swampy country of
the "leeks" at the eighth and ninth! How icy was the first
trickle that definitely insinuated itself between the collar and
the neck! How slippery grew our grips, and how puddingy the
soft faces of our drivers, battered by the flint-hearted gutty!
Our clothes had golden streaks on them where we had tried to
wipe off the sand from our fingers after teeing the ball, and I
seem to remember tipping up the tee box in the vain hope of
finding sand that was less like treacle. If there were no puddles
in the boxes, there certainly was one at the crater green, where,
indeed, we were lucky if we could hole out. Still, that was the
fifteenth; we were getting near home by that time, and the
sensation of noble endurance, which had only just kept us
alive at the turn, was now making us throw out our chests
and think that this was the sort of thing which had made
Englishmen what they were. Soon came the changing into the
clothes which had got wet the day before and were now dry
with many strange crinkles in them, and then the tea. I suppose
that, after all, it was rather good fun, though I am afraid that
this time I shall not have the courage—but then, of course,
this time it will not rain.

It was largely these egotistical memories that put rainy golf
into my head, but there was something else as well, a more
unselfish and admirable something. I have been reading at
full length the accounts of the American Open Championship,
of which I had only before heard by cable, and there were
some truly heroic things done at Winged Foot in the rain.
There was, for instance, Mr. Bobby Jones's second round,
which went far towards winning him the Championship.
Having begun with a sixty-nine, he had to set out on his

second round in something described as a waterspout. American writers sometimes exaggerate our winds into hurricanes because they are not very well used to golfing winds, but they know all about rain, and are not likely to use over-strong language about it. So I am sure this was real rain, and, moreover, it went on spouting throughout the whole round. Yet the crowd followed the great Bobby all the way—a piece of wonderful bravery in itself—and he went round in seventy-five. This sounds quite magnificent, and no doubt it was, but it was nothing to what Mr. von Elm did in the same storm. He got so wet that he had to strip his shirt off in the middle of the round, and the greens became so waterlogged that he putted with his mid-iron, and yet he finished in seventy. In the circumstances, this may have been one of the greatest rounds ever played.

American golfers seem to be capable of astonishing achievements in the rain. The second day's play in the qualifying round of the American Championship at Brookline in 1922 was one of the wettest I ever saw. The flat expanse of the polo ground, over which the first and last holes are played, was a series of pools divided by pathways of grass; the players had hard work to find anything like a dry putt to the hole between the puddles, no matter how skilfully they lifted; the rain came down and went on coming down in buckets. Yet Mr. Guilford went round in a record score of seventy, and I think Mr. Evans had a seventy-two and Mr. Jones a seventy-three. These rain-defying champions seem to possess no particular secret except an iron determination to make the best of things. They strap towels to their belts, wind cotton wrappings round the grips of their clubs or put on cotton gloves, and then out they go in their thin shirts and linen knickerbockers. They are drenched to the skin before they have finished the first hole, and they go round in seventy!

"You don't seem to mind it," observed Bob Sawyer, as he and Sam sat half-drowned outside the postchaise.

"Vy, I don't exactly see no good my mindin' on it 'ud do, sir," replied Sam.

That, no doubt, is the right spirit, and I will endeavour to emulate it, but really, if it comes to shirts, I think I shall stay indoors. One must draw the line somewhere.

A LITTLE SCOTTISH PARADISE

There is a Scottish course which has many charms, but no fame at all. I am not even prepared to say that it is a good one, but I will say that I never think of it without wishing I was there. This little Paradise—for it is only a short course—is private, and I am not going to mention its name lest the owner should never ask me to play there again. I will call it merely "K", and pass the reader no more than this hint, that it is a few miles from one of the most celebrated of all links, where there is no play on a Sunday. Consequently, it is on a Sunday afternoon that we go to play there, and I imagine it during all the rest of the week lying utterly solitary amid its woods. In the morning we read the murders and the cricket in the Sunday papers, make a supreme effort, in the shape of the traditional walk to the burn and back again, have a short sleep, and reduce our bag of clubs to its lowest possible terms—let us say a driver, a mid-iron, a mashie and a putter. Then we have lunch, we pack ourselves and our skeleton army of clubs into a car and off we go. After crossing the narrowest of all stone bridges we turn off to the right; we go past the little old church with a Norman window which we are always intending to look at and never do; we turn to the right again on to the worst piece of road of my acquaintance, which brings all conversation to a standstill by its jolting. Soon we come into sandy country, a wonderful stretch of it with its bunkers ready-made; then we turn in where some farm buildings stand by a fir wood, and there we are.

Sometimes there are no other cars there, sometimes there are one or two, and sometimes even half a dozen, in which case we complain that the course will be unduly crowded. We walk down a path through the firs and the full beauties of the course burst upon us. It always reminds me of the similarly ecstatic moment of coming to Archerfield. There is the same delicious loneliness, the same feeling of being curtained by woods. "It's a bonny wee place," said my small caddie from Gullane when he first saw Archerfield. "You can see nothing but the rabbits and their wee white tails." And his words always come back to me as my feet first sink into the soft turf at K. There is no question of caddies here. We each have our own bag—a light canvas one if we are wise—and set out straightway to play one of the most alarming short holes I know. Technically, I believe, it is not the first hole; it is, in fact, the last or ninth, and just beyond it stands the club-house, a small hut of wood, reputed to contain secreted bottles of beer for those who know where to find them. However, it is the first hole we come to, and so we have to play it, 140 yards or so to a tiny green set on a devilish slope and guarded by a pond full of rushes. To get over the pond is a great thing; to get on to the green is a greater one; to get down in two putts when you are on the green is the greatest of all, an event so unlikely that you need scarcely consider it. I have had putts for two there, but I doubt if I have ever laid them dead, and I like best to be given the hole by an opponent who has gone into the pond.

After this tremendous beginning, K lets us down easily for a while. At the next hole there are no ponds, only rough grass at the sides and a rudimentary little bunker or two, and the holes are of that length which on other courses we should dismiss scornfully as a "drive and a chip". Indeed, we always think on the teeing ground that we ought to be able to drive the green; but the ground is not helpful and we are not quite so good as we think, and somehow we never do reach it. Even so, we fondly imagine that we ought to do a three, and yet we often do a five. The green is exceedingly small and rather hard and bumpy; the ground in front of it is exceedingly soft, so that if we try a pitch, we run over, and if we try a run-up, we pitch and stop. There are several holes of this type, presenting no extraordinary or, at any rate, no orthodox difficulties; but there are others that test us to the full. There is the third, for instance, a really fine one-shotter of the length of a good spoon shot, to an exiguous, slopy, bumpy plateau, with the fir wood behind and a bunker on either side. And then there is the sixth, only a hundred yards long, where the owner is prepared to give a brand new ball to the man who, on his first visit, can hole it in three. The last time I was there, by the way, two visitors qualified for this reward, but the owner had prudently disappeared when, full of expectations, they finished their round. Certainly, it is the trickiest little beast of a hole, with a ditch—no, a burn—in front and thick grass all round and a fence so near on the left-hand side that it is quite easy to go out of bounds even with a mashie niblick. The eighth, too, is a good one, with its tempting tee shot over a corner and its second over a patch of rushes. Have I not put three balls in succession out of bounds from that tee and lost them all? Grand shots they were, too, all three of them, suffering only from a touch too much of a brave and virile hook. Oh no, I assure you, K is not so easy as it looks.

The perils of the course do not all come from the hand of Nature. Man contributes to them in that he always appears to be driving straight at our devoted heads. The holes criss-cross one another in the manner of a cat's cradle, and the ordinary etiquette of golf is somewhat relaxed. We give one yell and then we drive at our neighbour, and he does the same by us; *sauve qui peut!* There is one putting green that serves for two holes, and in that case there has to be a certain amount of give and take as to which match shall hole out first. Nobody seems to get killed, and, indeed, some of the players whom I have seen on the course would not hurt you very much if they did hit you. It may be inferred from what I have said that K is not the course for the most serious kind of golf, and too much of it might, perhaps, be enervating, as giving us an excessive notion of our powers of doing fours. Yet golf there can be almost painfully exciting. On my last visit a friend and I had the temerity to match our worst ball against so august a personage as a Provost. It was a desperate fight, and we ought certainly to have been beaten, but "by the damdest providence", as old Mr. Blackwood used to say, the Provost missed his putt.

I do not know when I shall next go there, but this I do know, that, if I am anywhere near it, wild horses will not keep me away. I shall think about it as I get to King's

Cross—absurdly early, as one always gets to the station on any journey that has a touch of romance about it. I shall think about it as I lie wakeful in my berth, listening to the clanking of the wheels over the metals.

ADVENTURES WITH AN ARCHITECT

"I had no keener pleasure than in following Holmes in his professional investigations, and in admiring the rapid deductions, as swift as intuitions, and yet always founded on a logical basis, with which he unravelled the problems which were submitted to him."

This was, in effect, what I said, in the manner of Dr. Watson, as I bade good-bye to an eminent golfing architect after spending two exciting days in his company. It was, in some ways, a rather humbling experience, though I really am very humble, anyhow as regards my architectural qualities; but the feeling of being a foil to Holmes's brilliance was by no means disagreeable. If the architect could see some things more quickly than I could, and other things which I should never have seen at all, I could console myself with the reflection that it was his job. It was only natural that he should be good at it, and that seems a point worth emphasising, because there are sometimes members of green committees who think that they can do this job by the light of nature, and they generally make the saddest mess of it.

For the moment I must not say on what course we were working, but if I give a clue here and there and somebody recognises it, I suppose no fatal harm will be done. Several of us had been appointed on a sub-committee to try to devise alterations—the fewest and cheapest possible—that should make less perilous a road that runs through the course. One or two long-cherished holes had to go; that could not be helped. We took as our motto that we did not mind hitting each other, but we must not hit the passer-by. We toiled amain and produced a scheme, and then we asked our architect to come and look. He had not seen the course for twenty years, but, with the aid of a plan, he had, in the seclusion of his own room, designed something uncommonly like our scheme. That was cheering, but it made us wonder if we were quite so clever as we had thought. As we walked round with him we wondered more and more.

It was not that he said to us with Holmesian sarcasm: "You are scintillating to-day, my dear Watson." Far from it; in a general way he approved of us, but—confound the fellow!—how quickly he did improve on us too! Our new first hole, for instance, hugging the sandhills, with a tee shot from a height, he blessed entirely, but he found a far better green than we had only twenty yards away. Why in the world hadn't we seen it? I am sure I don't know. Our architect made straight for it with ecstatic cries. "Look at it," he exclaimed, "it's perfect. Look at the slopes and folds, and oh! look at the lovely drop into the little valley behind."

After this, nothing much happened for a while. Our architect nobly restrained some beautiful imaginings that were out of the question and only polished most efficiently our crudities. Presently, however, we came to a really big problem, a new ninth hole in more or less virgin country. "There," we said to him, half-proudly, half-tremulously. "We thought of going down that valley", and we showed him a shallow valley of broken, benty, sandy ground which we had fondly likened to some pretty holes at Formby or Birkdale and to one at Prince's. "No," said the great man. "No. That bores me": and then in gentler tones, "you know I don't want to insult anyone, but you chose that because it was obvious." It was true, and we felt like little boys who had been caught using a crib in school. The valley, he said, gave the player a feeling of confidence; he felt that those banks to right and left would keep him in the proper path, and so he could hit out boldly, just as a man does in approaching a green with a back or side wall to it. That was dull; the thing to engender in the player's breast was doubt and wondering, not confidence. In the end he had to come back to our poor, despised hole. I readily admit he improved on it, because he managed to turn the second shot partially out of the valley. At the same time, we did feel like the Doctor when, for once in a while, he mildly scored, and Holmes remarked: "A hit, my dear Watson, a palpable hit."

I will not go all the way round and tell of the blessing of our new tees to the tenth and the eighteenth, nor of his new one-shot seventeenth, of almost idyllic simplicity, which he believes will be a beauty. I will pass on to the second day, when the architect and I went out again, accompanied by one caddie and one chauffeur, who had so many things strapped round him that he looked like a ticket collector on a 'bus. They carried maps, compasses, mackintoshes and other fearsome instruments of which I did not understand the purpose. I felt like an old lady in one of John Leach's *Punch* pictures. She thought that a party of R.Es were aiming at her with a blunderbuss, and had to be reassured with the words: "Don't be alarmed, ma'am, it's only a dumpy leveller." In these mathematical rites I took no part, but I did something. I carried three clubs round, and at intervals was bidden to play a shot to show, as I suppose, where the reasonably competent drive of a middle-aged gentleman would finish. The architect generally walked some forty yards past my ball, stuck his shooting-stick in the ground and said: "Right. Then here is the tiger's tee shot." Still, I had my compensating moments. He declared that from the new tenth tee I could not reach the seventeenth green (which, thank goodness, will have to go), and I banged the ball not merely on to that green, but over it.

If anyone has ever tried this game of hitting shots to order for the purpose of particular tests, he will agree with me that it is no easy task, producing a horrible self-consciousness. You are told, for example, to hold the ball up as far as you can to the right: this with a wind blowing from right to left. You do it only too thoroughly, and produce a short slice. "Did you hit it?" yells the architect in the distance. "I could get farther with a little hook," you shout back reproachfully, and are told to try again. On the whole, I did uncommonly well. Only once did he design a pot bunker exactly where my best ball lay; I must add that he is splendidly economical in bunkers. Once—at least once—he had to reconsider his tee because my drive had gone too far, and—proudest honour of all—my shot with a driver and a teed ball was accepted as a real tiger's brassy shot.

After some two and a half hours with driver and dumpy leveller, we returned to the club-house, and never did I sink more gratefully into a chair or consume with greater zest, what Mr. Swiveller called a modest quencher. If anybody thinks that golfing architects do not work hard and earn their living by the sweat of their brow, I hereby throw down my gauntlet and will meet him with niblicks. That is to say, when I have recovered. I must have a little rest first.

PROVIDENCE AND POLITENESS

A and B were coupled together the other day in a team match played by foursomes. Said A to B before they started: "You mustn't mind my being very short. I'm getting old and I can't hit hard—but I shall be all right when I get on the greens." He is as truthful a man as he is a modest one; he is, as a rule, a capital putter, and was really justified in what he said. Yet can anyone, who has experienced the singular malignancy of the golfing fates, have the least doubt what occurred? Of course he cannot. The tragedy is so inevitable as hardly to be worth setting down; on this particular day poor A had a series of putts of four and five feet on icy, slippery greens, and the ball would *not* go into the hole.

It is rash to say—whether to your partner or to anyone else—"Well, anyhow, I'm driving well—that won't let me down," or alternatively: "I can't get very far, but I can keep the ball in play." It would be much wiser to keep to yourself the fact that you feel thoroughly confident with your iron clubs. Yet in both these cases the fates may forgive you. Whatever you do, you must never say that you can putt, for then you will not be forgiven. There is nobody in the world who is a good enough putter to be able to prophesy that on this particular day he will putt well. He may do so on every other day in the year, but this will be the one day on which something goes wrong. There are a few fortunate mortals who never drive badly, but there is no such thing as an entirely trustworthy putter, nor would there be if the hole were made as big as a soup plate. *Nemo omnibus horis sapit*, which means that everybody misses the short ones sometimes. Most of us have learnt our lesson and go out of our way to avoid tempting Providence. When we meet another match and ask the players how they are getting on, the man who is down will answer candidly enough, sometimes, indeed, ostentatiously

magnifying the extent of the disaster; but the man who is
leading will be tongue-tied and embarrassed. He will take
refuge in generalities, such as that he is not doing so badly so
far, or that he is a little up at present; if he is tactlessly pressed
to give details he will make mysterious signs with his fingers,
twisting himself into such a position that his adversary cannot
see what he is doing. He does this partly from politeness, in
that he does not want to appear to be chortling at his enemy's
expense, but this is but a superficial motive compared with
that deeply implanted fear of the Nemesis that waits for
boasters; he is far more afraid of the evil chance than he is of
bad manners.

Some while ago two small boys were playing a match in a
juvenile competition. Near the turn one of them held a cheering lead of three. At that moment enters to him a small sister,
who calls to him: "How are you getting on, George?" The
leader, scarlet with embarrassment and looking at his opponent out of the corner of his eye, mutters that he is "all
right." "Yes, but how's the match?" calls the sister, more
shrilly; and again he answers, more uncomfortable than ever:
"I'm all right." "How many up are you?" this time screams the
relentless young lady, and then she proclaims to an invisible
somebody in the background: "Hurrah! George is three up!
Three up! He's going to win." Poor George did win in the
end, but he suffered terribly in doing so, and probably told
his sister very forcibly afterwards that these things were not
done.

It is arguable that at golf we take too much pains to try to
conceal our feelings (we do not do it very well, nevertheless),
and that it would be better to be as simple and natural as
was that young lady. An entirely inexperienced spectator
sometimes feels inclined to shout with joy when the enemy
misses a putt or goes into a bunker, but the indignant faces
that look round at him from among his neighbours freeze the
cheer upon his lips. I do not wish it to be otherwise, for golf
is sufficiently agonising and exasperating without that added
horror. I am only reflecting how differently we behave when
we are watching golf as compared with some other game.
When somebody shoots at an open goal and misses, no
chivalry prevents a fierce roar of joy and relief going up to

Heaven, neither does it when our man ought to have been run out by yards and has been saved by a glorious muddle on the part of the fielder or the wicket-keeper. These two instances are comparable to that of a man missing a short putt, and yet we yell in the one case and stand in solemn and hypocritical silence in the other. It is, I suppose, largely because in golf the player's tragedy is entirely of his own making; his adversary has had nothing whatever to do with it; whereas in cricket we may say that we do not cheer because the enemy batsman has missed the ball, but because our own heroic bowler has hit the wicket. Also, in golf the spectators are so near to the player that there would be something particularly brutal in their cheering his misfortunes while standing right over him. We cannot, in moments of tension, help gloating, but there is something indecent in the notion of letting him see us.

This delicacy of deportment on the part of golfers leads to an odd difference in the scenes that follow the end of a big match. When a player has a putt for the match and holes it there goes up a splendid and spontaneous shout which does the heart good to hear; but when he has a putt to save the match and misses it, things can never be the same. There comes a perceptible pause, then someone begins to clap, and finally the clapping comes in scattered and irregular volleys; but the first fine rapture of community cheering is unattainable. If the putt missed is painfully short, it is impossible to make any great demonstration, no matter how fervently we have been wishing it missed. Even in a scoring competition the nature of the stroke with which the victor ends his labours makes all the difference. There is no more exciting moment than that in which the winner of the Open Championship makes his way through the crowd round the last green, flag-bearers and stewards forcing a passage for him, to consummate his triumph; but we shout much more loudly if the last stroke is actually a good one. When Hagen came to the seventy-second hole at Muirfield in 1929 he was, humanly speaking, certain to win; we were all ready to cheer him with our whole souls, for he had played magnificently. He put his second in a bunker and then played a typically beautiful shot out to within four or five feet of the pin. Now we were all a-tiptoe, and if he had holed that putt, as he nearly always would, what a yell there would have been! But he missed it, gave a little smile and shake of his head, and then tapped the ball in from two inches. Of course, we all cheered, but the supreme moment had passed without being seized and could not be recaptured. Sometimes, too, it happens on these occasions that the winner has to hole his putt first and then his obscure and neglected partner has to putt. That is bad stage management on the part of fate, and robs the scene of a perceptible part of its thrill.

A good many years ago I saw what seemed then, and still seems to me a curious scene in the Ladies' Championship. There was a really splendid match between two most illustrious ladies. One of them was dormy one, and after each had played three shots their balls lay almost equidistant—some four feet—from the hole. The one who was dormy putted first and holed. That was the match; I uttered an excited squeak which was just going to turn into a shout when fierce female eyes glowered at me on all sides and I subsided, crushed. There was not a sound and nobody moved a muscle until the loser had also holed her four-foot putt in order to say that she was one down and not two down. Honesty as to short putts is certainly a virtue, but this was carrying it to a pitch of which I had never dreamed. However, I am not a heroic lady, but only a weak, erring man who likes to say he is as few holes down as he decently can.

THE KNOT IN THE HANDKERCHIEF

Our Ryder Cup team, after a hard course of tournaments, have now vanished into a mysterious and exciting seclusion. I gather that they are at Harrogate. Whether they are drinking waters with "a wery strong flavour o' warm flat irons" I do not know, though there would seem to be something vaguely appropriate in it if they were. Whatever their precise form of training, I feel tolerably sure that they are not, occult from the public eye, practising with handkerchiefs tied into knots.

It is perhaps too late in the day to suggest it to them; yet a gentleman of my acquaintance has found in this apparently simple device the twin secrets of driving and happiness. He had played golf of a kind for years before he was suddenly smitten with a desire for indoor self-improvement. Fluffy woollen balls and india-rubber balls brought him no relief; then he tied the knot in his handkerchief, shut himself up with a library of text-books, and emerged after a time a creature changed and radiant.

I went to see him in his office the other day, that he might show me how it was done. It was a solemn moment when he took from a drawer a large plain white handkerchief. He rolled it up till it looked like a very long attenuated sausage. Swiftly and surely he tied a knot in it, and yet another knot, and now it resembled—more or less—a golf ball with two aeroplane wings attached. He repeated the process with another handkerchief, and our supply of ammunition was complete. Then he hesitated a moment. However, it was past one o'clock, there was no one about, and even a senior partner can do what he likes with his own luncheon hour. He picked up a driver from the corner, and stealthily we crept out on to the landing. Not a mouse stirred behind the wainscot; all was well; he put one handkerchief on the ground to act as a tee, and the other handkerchief on the top of it, the aeroplane wings pointing in the direction of the imaginary hole. Finally, with the air of a priest taking the sacrificial knife, he grasped his driver. I retired to the safety of the staircase to look on.

At this supreme juncture there came a most untimely interruption. Steps were heard on the staircase—the steps of Miss Somebody returning to work after all too short a lunch. "Come along, Miss Somebody," said my friend blandly, as if he were doing the most ordinary thing in the world, and with an embarrassed smile she plunged through the nearest glass door. Silence reigned once more, but only for an instant. Bang! there came a noise like a pistol shot. He had swung his driver round his head and the handkerchief had hurled itself against the wall. "There!" he cried proudly, and I, like Mr. Wemmick's aged parent, when the cannon went off, exclaimed: "He's fired! I heerd him!" But I had missed something of the point. The striker's exulting gaze was directed not at the handkerchief against the wall, but at the other one upon the ground. There it had remained, immovable and untouched, even as the face of the trusting spectator's watch from which Kirkwood drives his ball. The achievement was complete.

After that we went to lunch, and a very good one we had. I carried away with me one of the handkerchiefs tied by the master hand, and shall no more dare untie it than I dare unroll my umbrella when an artist has rolled it for me. I have, however, ventured to hit it, because before writing this plain and unvarnished tale I thought I ought to have a little trial on my own account. I admit, however, that I felt cramped and frightened in the drawing-room, and so began by taking it on to the lawn. It whizzed away satisfactorily enough, but I could not make quite the same splendid bang with it as its creator had done. It may have been my puny hitting, or it may be that the real reverberating sound can only be obtained within four walls.

I may seem to have written lightly, almost frivolously, of this adventure, but in fact the knot in the handkerchief is, I believe, a capital device. One thing is certain, that it is much better to practise swinging at something than at nothing. When we swing merely at the empty air we may look like all the photographs of all the champions, and get our knees and our elbows into exactly the right places, but there is absent one intensely important element—namely, that of timing. With nothing to aim at, we are much more likely—and Heaven knows we are likely enough when there is a real ball—to hit too soon. "Wait for it" is one of the eternal imperatives of golf; we cannot wait for nothing, but we can wait for a handkerchief.

I cross-examined my friend rather sternly about hooking and slicing, since it seemed to me that he might be acquiring bad habits in one of these two directions without knowing it. He made some admissions, but came back to the solid, satisfying fact that he had found out how to drive a golf ball after being unable to do so for almost unnumbered years. I only wish I had half his complaint.

Crash! bang! That was the genuine note. I have left that blessed handkerchief in the hall, and somebody else has had a shot at it. It sounds—it really does sound—as if he had broken something.

INCHES AND ELLS

"Well, you knew it was there. You ought to have gone somewhere else." That is the answer that we have often made, not perhaps aloud but in the recesses of our own minds, to an adversary bemoaning a ball which has just trickled into an unkind bunker, or just hopped out of bounds. No doubt also our enemy has often made it to us when it has been our turn to call gods and men to witness the gross unfairness of the world.

It played its part in a discussion during the Easter holidays, which were so much better suited to talking about golf than to playing it. There were four of us, and one, who has the power of life and death at a particular course, invited our considered judgments as to whether the fourth hole would be better if the penalty for out of bounds were reduced from stroke and distance to the loss of distance only. We all had the conviction that he would do what he thought best in his dictatorial mind, whatever our opinions might be, but still we were flattered at being asked. So we did our best, and, as in the case of the three jovial huntsmen, the first said one thing and the second another, and "the other he said nay". A wanted to make the penalty half a stroke and all the distance, and we all shouted him down. He protested that he did not see why it was impossible, but we just said: "Away with it," and gave no reasons. B wanted to keep the rule as it is—namely, the rule of golf, which prescribes the loss of stroke and distance; but he admitted a sneaking desire to keep the full penalty only when the hole was played from the back tee, and to be more lenient in the case of the forward tee. His *ratio decidendi*, if I have the expression aright, was that the longer the hole the better the chance of catching up, whereas at a shorter hole the full penalty almost inevitably meant the loss of the hole. Then came my turn, and I began by trying to sit on the fence. I said that as there were so few chances of going out of bounds on this particular course, I thought the full penalty should be retained; if it had been Hoylake, where there are almost endless possibilities, loss of distance was enough. I was proceeding to add an interesting story about a friend of mine who, in the course of an ill-spent life, had been out of bounds at every single hole at Hoylake except the Rushes, when I was brought ruthlessly back to the point. The dictator said to me, as Mr. Pickwick did to Sam on the shooting expedition: "Kindly reserve your anecdotes till they are called for." What he wanted to know was whether this single hole would be better under one rule or under the other.

I was frightened nearly out of my wits and tried to think not what was my own truthful opinion but what was the answer he would like. He is a gentleman of strongly conservative views, a hater of local rules, and I could hardly imagine that he would allow any concession to southern weaknesses. But in that case what was there in his vast and brooding mind, and why had he asked us the question? Finally, stammering and blushing, I voted for loss of distance only, and—I had guessed right. He admitted that he stood aghast at his own moderation, that his views had undergone a surprising change, and that he now thought that the hole would be "better sport" under the milder penalty. That being so, I presume the rule will be altered, and the next time that I, too greatly daring, try to lay down my tee shot between that magnetic little pot bunker in the middle of the course and the railway line on the right, I shall play not three from the tee but two.

I have been wondering since whether he and I—for what I am worth, which is very little—are right. It is a difficult question. At present if the player who has the honour goes out of bounds he will probably take six to the hole, and the other man, by a series of more or less ignominious scuffles and scrambles to the left, can comfortably get his five and win the hole; only the truly heroic on one side, or the ineffably futile on the other, can prevent such an ending; when the first ball soars away on to the railway line the hole is to all intents and purposes over. On the other side there is that good old solid argument that the player knows the railway is there and goes near it at his peril. Is there not something more besides, a consideration not merely of hard justice but of natural, human pleasure? At present, if I can steer my ball close to the railway I derive from the feat a positively glowing satisfaction. And, alternatively, if I pull away safely to the left I can still pat myself on the back for having used my head and refused to be tempted to my destruction. It is the imminence of the peril, the terrible severity of the punishment avoided, that give to my feelings such a delicious poignancy. In proportion as the peril and the punishment are decreased so will my blissful relief be decreased also, for to fear death is truly to taste the joys of living.

The hole in question—you can see it from the train on your way to Southampton—is in design and conception very like the sixteenth hole at St. Andrews. If my friend held that gorgeous hole in fee, would he, I wonder, contemplate reducing the penalty for going into the railway there to loss of distance only? He would not. His conservative instincts would be too much for him. It might possibly be inconsistent, but that would not matter. He would take the strong line, and afterwards, like Frederick the Great, would find some pedant to point out why he was right. Right, in my humble judgment, he would be. To flout the railway and the Principal's Nose, to forget all about Deacon Sime and to fare unscathed down that narrow way, gives to life a zest so intense that surely nothing should be allowed to diminish it. No, when I think of the Corner of the Dyke, I am all for the rigour of the game, and almost hope that my friend may return to his older and fiercer opinions.

There is no fear of his growing in a general way too mild, for on another point he was once more the man of granite. One of the company, B, encouraged by his comparatively melting mood, complained of the severity of the bunker behind the green at the seventh—a one-shot hole requiring an iron shot of some length and accuracy. B soon had cause to regret his ill-judged temerity. It was pointed out to him, first, that the bunker was a "protective" one, and that but for it a worse thing would befall him and his ball be unplayable in a gorse bush; secondly, that if he could not get out of the bunker he ought to be ashamed of himself, that his niblick should be broken and he himself scourged off the links with

what remained of the shaft. Finally, when we got to that
green, we spent some time letting balls trickle as gently as
possible over the edge and having it triumphantly demon-
strated to us that no ball could possibly remain under the
bank. When some people give you inches, it does not pay to
ask for ells.

STRIPPING FOR ACTION

You cannot teach an old dog new tricks, but if the dog is going to have apoplexy unless he learns the trick you must at least from motives of common humanity try to teach him.

This observation is produced by the hot weather. Some time ago I played in a two-day match, and, together with one other old dog, I played, as is my custom, in a coat, while the other fourteen players engaged played more or less in their shirt-sleeves. At the end of the two days I was so entirely prostrated that two alternatives presented themselves. Either to learn to play in shirt-sleeves or give up midsummer golf.

It is not, if an egotistical explanation may be pardoned, that I have any violently Tory views about coatlessness. During two summers I played on the torrid marshes of the Vardar in khaki shirts which turned canary coloured from the sunshine, but I never grew accustomed to a garb which seemed to increase, from its unnatural freedom, a natural slice. Safe at home again, I put on a nice, tight, grey flannel coat, and this was no mere gesture, such as the shaving off of a moustache, to show that adjutant-generals had ceased to trouble; it was a serious attempt to cure that slice, and it produced for a while a blessed tendency to hook. Since then I have flirted once or twice with jerseys and jerkins, but have always swung myself into such complicated knots that the coat had to be resumed. But now something must be done. What the Americans can learn to do, surely an Englishman can learn too. "Whereby," as Jack Bunsby remarked, "Why not? If so, what odds? Can any man say otherwise? No. Awast then!"

That the art of playing without a coat does require some learning there is surely no doubt. The delicious sense of freedom is full of perils and can produce terrific errors. Two venerable gentlemen of my acquaintance were watching the match that I mentioned, and, as the ball went flying into the rough, one of them remarked that when he used to take part in the match people did not play like that. The other, essentially more charitable, suggested that perhaps it was that the players were suffering from having suddenly taken their coats off. He received only an angry snort in reply, but he may have been right; it is tolerably certain, at any rate, that not for a long time have so many good golfers hit the ball so often and so far into such luxuriant hay.

On the other hand, this freedom may have its advantages, if only the player realises its dangers. He is put on his guard against swinging too fast and too far; he is extremely conscious of the temptation to hurry, and by taking measures against it may even attain to a smoothness and rhythm of which he has hitherto only dreamed. If he is not so sinuous or so slim as he used to be, he will be surprised to find the club-head coming once more within his range of vision at the top of the swing. That will gratify him as he remembers that Bobby Jones has said that Britons do not swing far enough, but he must not presume on his new-found joy, or he will spin round like an insane teetotum on the way down and "pivot" himself to glory and the grave. While not forgetting the words of the American sage, he should also recall those of a Scottish one:—"A good swing seems to the onlooker swift and flexible; but if the player feels supple he exhibits an awkward, stiff, straggling movement. The player ought to be, in his own hands, a stiff bow which he bends and shoots with."

With my head full of these and other wise maxims I went to a sequestered valley to practise. When I got there I took off my coat, but, if I may delicately allude to them, I retained my braces in order to begin by degrees. The solitude of the valley was not quite so complete as in my self-consciousness I could have wished. There were one or two assiduous ladies thumping their way round, card in hand, and the lines of an old cricket poem jingled themselves in my head.

Each nymph looks askance at her favourite swain,
And views him half-stripped with both pleasure and pain.

Luckily they were quite inappropriate, for I did not know the ladies and they showed no interest whatever in me. Still, it was pleasanter when they disappeared and I teed my ball on the brink of the great adventure. The first few shots gave me a sensation of having drunk some elixir of youth, but then I knew they would; so had the first strokes in the jerseys and jerkins, flattering only most horribly to deceive. I was trying to imitate the Americans, and clearly I must behave as they would, hitting hundreds of balls and not stopping pusillanimously after a few respectable shots. Looking at it as if it belonged to somebody else, I thought there was really something almost heroic in that solitary figure tramping up and down the valley under a broiling sun. The ladies reappeared, having thumped several holes, and vanished again, and still the figure toiled on, nor were its efforts by any means unsuccessful. The litheness and grace of its follow-through positively compelled my admiration; the ball, with the sun-burnt ground to help it, went considerable distances and decently straight. Only after an hour and a half of solid slogging did the figure pick up its coat and climb very slowly out of the valley and up the hill. It looked decidedly limp but not unhappy.

Goodness only knows I am not puffed up; the battle is not won yet, for practice is one thing and a game quite another, and I shall be terribly frightened when first I face an enemy without my trusty coat. In any case, slicing must be presumed to be preferable to dying, though this is open to argument. The question of removing the braces is at the moment in abeyance. After all, William Lillywhite bowled in them and Fuller Pilch batted in them, and that ought to be enough for humbler folk.

ON STANDING UP TO IT

There is a friend of mine, a good Scottish golfer, who has been all his life a consistent scoffer at theories. If he has, as I suspect, some little private remedies and beliefs of his own, he never reveals them. The only recipe for hitting the ball which I have ever heard fall from his lips is: "Stand up and give it one."

The other day I watched a player who came nearer to obeying this simple and comprehensive piece of advice than anyone I had ever seen before. He played very well, easily, gracefully and without pressing, but the point about him is this, that he is the only good golfer whom I have ever seen stand absolutely at his full height in addressing the ball. I have seen other people do it occasionally, but they were not good golfers; they were generally beginners who had not played other games; they looked as stiff and uncomfortable as a pair of compasses dressed in coat and trousers, and they missed the ball. This player of mine, on the other hand, looked perfectly at ease and not in the least stiff. Yet, there he was, standing bolt upright. How he could do it while other people cannot do it I do not know, but it occurred to me that he would make a good text for a discourse against crouching. This, coming from me, is Satan rebuking Sin with a vengeance, for I have long known that I look like one of those very old cab horses still sometimes to be seen in a drowsy fly at some quiet, sunshiny little station in the country. Indeed, I have given up the effort to look like anything else, but the most hardened criminal may effectively point out the errors of their ways to other criminals, and so I cry, as one calling to repentance: "Why do we crouch?"

Our old friend Sir Walter Simpson is nearly always worth looking up, and here is what he said on the subject: "The most natural manner in which to address a ball is, of course, to stand with legs straight and firm, and with no more stoop of the body than is absolutely necessary to enable the player to see it with straight eyes. But golfers, good ones, in the laudable endeavour to stand well away from the ball, acquire in great numbers the habit of stooping forward more than is necessary. These instinctively apply a corrective. For instance, some bend their knees. There are extremists who even stoop so far forward, and have cancelled the effect of doing so to such an extent by bending their knees, that they would fit a chair, if placed behind them when driving. Other good players who stoop over their work keep their bodies steady and their grip of the ground firm by placing the left foot nearer the line of fire than the right." He went on to prophesy that which came true, that some day there would be illustrious players who would "cancel their stoop" by putting the left foot back and the right foot forward.

I wonder if Sir Walter was right in saying that it was natural to stand up. It might be cogently argued that it is natural to sit down because we feel, quite erroneously, that the nearer we get to the ball the more likely we are to hit it. Otherwise, why is it—and I think the fact is beyond question—that when we get nervous or anxious we creep in on the ball? Not only do we not stand well away from it, but we do not stand well up to it. Personally, I know only too well the sensation of my nose getting closer to the ball in a crisis, and I have observed the same phenomenon in others, and that not only in short shots, but in those intended to be long.

Whatever the reason for our crouching, there can be little doubt that it is a criminal act. We are more likely to lose our balance, and various parts of our anatomy, especially our elbows, are more likely to fly out and get in the way. We cannot be free in our hitting, and freedom is a great virtue. Moreover, our bodies are not such fools as we are, and they try to remedy our faults on their own account. Therefore, though we start doubled up, our bodies take the law into their own hands and try to straighten themselves up in the middle of the swing, with horrific results. Braid has said somewhere that most amateurs have an unconquerable inclination to let their bodies move upwards just at the moment of hitting an iron shot, and that it is this habit that goes far to make them the bad iron players that they undoubtedly are. Clearly we should be less inclined to do so if we stood reasonably well up to begin with.

A good deal must depend on the individual golfer's figure. It is easier for a short man to stand well up to his ball than a tall one. Mr. Bobby Jones is certainly not tall, and he stands up magnificently. Indeed, when I said that I had never seen anyone do so as well as the player whom I took for my text, I am not sure that I ought not to have excepted the quadruple champion. Mr. Hilton, again, is comparatively short, and he, too, like the heroes of old novels with curling lips and scornful eyes, used to "draw himself up to his full height". On the other hand, take an exceptionally tall man, Jim Barnes, and you will see that he, by comparison, stoops, but you will also see how admirably he cancels any disadvantage of doing so by keeping his body at the same angle throughout the stroke. There is no suspicion of a lift at the moment of hitting, and he finishes the stroke with his body still kept rigidly down. In rather impolite language, which may yet give a valuable clue, he keeps his stomach tucked in throughout the stroke. Another famous croucher (I only use the word in a comparative sense in talking of these great ones) is Sandy Herd. He gets rid of his difficulties in a characteristic way of his own, because he not only perceptibly sways his body to the right in the back swing, but also lifts it perceptibly upward. He does it, of course, with perfect rhythm and smoothness, but for other people to emulate that lift would be dangerous. It is less complicated and less perilous to stand up before the swing has started.

"Stand up" is one of the easiest pieces of advice in the world to give, but so is "Go in and win," and so was Dr. W. G. Grace's: "Put the bat against the ball," and one is nearly as hard to follow as either of the other two. Those of us who suffer from crouching are conscious on our good days that we are standing up better than usual, but when the bad days come round again we cannot do it by taking thought. I can still remember a happy summer holiday, nearly thirty years ago, when I used to repeat to myself: "Keep your d—d head as far away from the d—d ball as you can," and it worked like a charm. I never drove so well before or since, but, after the holiday, those blessed, if profane, words lost their magic, and no formula that I have ever invented since has worked as well. To stiffen the knees is one obvious cure, but after a successful shot or two they feel too stiff and we are undone. In fact, I do not believe that any catchword cure, if I may so term it, is of any use. The only way to make ourselves stand up is to stand up, and that is not a very helpful piece of wisdom.

THE BEGINNER

"The young of the penny whistler," as we know from one of the few unquestionably great works in English literature, "is occult from observation; he is never heard until proficient, or providence defends human hearing from his first attempts upon the upper octave."

It is otherwise with the young of the golfer, and so I told a lady of my acquaintance the other day when she announced her intention of beginning, or re-beginning, golf at a week-end on a popular course near London. She could never endure, she said, to drive off before a grinning mob and would find some quiet spot on the course where no eye but her Maker's could see her. This proposition struck me as so excessive that I made her promise to write and tell me how she had fared. The ensuing words are therefore substantially her own and form a very poignant story.

Fortune treated her scurvily. She and her play-fellow decided to start so that they should arrive in the middle of the morning, when as they fondly hoped, the teeing ground would be empty. Their car, however, declined to start, and only after some persuasion brought them to the course at luncheon time. Being hungry and exhausted they lunched, and when they had finished the tee was not empty; so there was nothing for it but to drive off, as she says, "before a *regiment* of impatient golfers, all with gleams of anticipation of her making a fool of herself very imperfectly disguised in their expressions." I pause for an instant to suggest that she flatters herself as to the amount of interest she aroused and will go on with the story. Her partner drove into a deep moat, and she into a mountain of dead leaves four yards from the tee. In this, with the aid of someone else's caddie, they burrowed feverishly, while the poor lady never ceased screaming "to the crowd of vultures" to go on. At length she found her ball and joined her partner in the moat. At this point there is a hiatus, but ultimately they ran, hot with shame, to the first green and decided that this would not do.

A luminous notion then struck them; they cut off a big slice of the course and found the fifteenth and sixteenth holes in solitude. These two holes run, it appears, parallel with one another, the one up a slope and the other down it. So they played these two holes as often as they could, marching up the hill and then down again like a couple of grand old Dukes of York. This part of the story affected me deeply, because I remembered how once upon a time, in extreme youth, I used thus to play not two but one hole over and over again. It was the old second hole at Felixstowe, and I used to take cover by the Martello tower and dash out whenever I saw a gap to play the hole between two pairs of grown-ups. Exactly how many times or in how many strokes they played their two holes I do not know; my deponent says that it reminded her of the rules for knitting—"hit one, miss two, drop one, miss three, &c,"—but she is sure that she once did one hole in five, "which is Bogey." They were ultimately caught up, but managed to slip in again to play the last two holes, and so finished in an entirely orthodox manner. In fact, as far as any casual passer-by could have told, they might have been Miss Leitch and Miss Wethered.

To her narrative my correspondent has appended certain conclusions about the game in general to which she has come. Golfing truths may be learnt from the mouths of golfing babes, and some of her remarks are both original and profound. She says, for instance, that she found almost unbearable the sensation of swinging the club up, because she felt that she would never be able to bring it down again. Now here surely is a new explanation of the reason why we all find it so hard to take the club back slowly enough. The real reason is clearly that without knowing it we suffer from this suppressed fear of not coming down again, and hurry accordingly. Then as regards the pitching she made quite by chance a discovery that should be useful to her through all her golfing life. No one would dare paraphrase Sir Isaac Newton, and it would be an impertinence for me to use any other words than her own. "Once," she says: "I was in *another* grassy moat and the ball was nestling in long coarse grass at an angle of forty-five degrees. I was *so* furious with it that I seized my mashie niblick as if it had been a woodman's axe and smote the ball with the intention of chopping it in half. It sailed into the air terrifically high and landed about two feet from the pin." What a lesson to us all! There in a sentence is the whole secret of hitting down on the ball with the iron shots and letting the club do the lofting.

Not so original, but not without interest, is the fact that the only long putt she holed all day was struck "negligently" and with the putter held in one hand. From this she concludes that: "It's no use trying. You must pull off a double bluff by deliberately pretending not to try to do what you want to do, or, alternatively, by not caring *what* happens." There succinctly expressed is the truth of which we have been mistily aware. Especially in the matter of short putts and little pitches over those odious cross bunkers. It remains to be seen whether this beginner is at the start of a great career as a golfer. Clearly she is already a great golfing philosopher.

A NOVICE'S ORDEAL

A correspondent has just stated an amusing problem to me in the following terms: "Can a normal person (male) reasonably proficient in other sports, but completely ignorant of golfing procedure and method, go round any eighteen-hole course in less than 200?" I quote the words as given to me because if the letter of the law were to be insisted upon in deciding the wager—and I gather there were several wagers—the exact words might be highly important. "Any eighteen-hole course" might cover anything between Ranelagh and Pine Valley, and the difference between these two is considerable. Moreover, the words matter so much more in the case of a complete beginner than in that of any ordinary golfer. Take, for instance, Sandwich and St. Andrews, two famous courses which to a good golfer present much the same degree of difficulty. St. Andrews would be in the nature of a paradise to the beginner, who could top, at any rate, a goodly number of shots with impunity. At Sandwich, on the other hand, he would top into big hills and chasms and would never get out again. If he took 200 strokes to St. Andrews, I should think he would take 300 to Sandwich. It appears that in this particular case the course was chosen by those who betted against the player, and was chosen with an eye to the number of its hazards. It was at Sorrento, which I take to be near Melbourne, for that is where the story comes from. Besides the main bet or bets there was a subsidiary one that the player would not, in the course of the round, hit a ball a distance of 200 yards in any direction, and whoever thought of that was a person of considerable astuteness, for the player's chief hope lay, as I should imagine, in not attempting too much.

And now for the game, which began, no doubt with a view

to a clear course, at half-past eight in the morning, Mr. H, the player, or, as my correspondent calls him, the "experimentee", being properly attired in the height—and width—of plus fours and liberally supplied with balls and clubs. He was closely watched by the opposing party, who reckoned up by his prospects as the round proceeded on the assumption that Bogey took eleven to each hole. If, then, he was two strokes worse than Bogey, he would fail; but to begin with he showed no signs whatever of failing, for he started with brilliant steadiness in 8, 6, 11, 7—one hole in exactly the Bogey score, the other three so far below it that "birdie" would most inadequately describe any of them. Unfortunately, I have no card of the course with the lengths of the holes, and therefore cannot say whether the six was more sparkling than the seven or whether, perhaps, the eleven was best of all. The opposition were feeling very glum until, at the fifth hole, something happened to cheer them. H at last got into serious trouble and "turned in a mediocre twenty-two". Still, even so, his score was one under elevens, and he pulled himself together to hole the next four holes in a total of forty-three, which brought him to the turn with something, but not a very large something, in hand.

H was, of course, by this time a vastly more experienced golfer than when he began, and so ought to have done better on the way home. On the other hand, I dare say he was also a less fresh and enthusiastic one and, furthermore, I am told that the homecoming nine holes are the harder. At any rate, he fell steadily behindhand, and when he holed out at the seventeenth his total was 205, and the bets were lost and won. With great bravery he got a nine to the eighteenth, and so finished in 214, 97 out and 117 home. He never did succeed in hitting that 200 yard drive, and as my correspondent observes (I am afraid he is a cunning fellow), "his earnest endeavours to fulfil this obligation materially contributed to his failure on the major issue." I wish I had more particulars to give of this remarkable achievement. I should very much like to know how many putts he took on the average and whether the bunkers cost him very dearly; but I am told none of these things. There is, however, a striking little piece of statistics which must have added one bitter ingredient to the cup of failure. H missed the globe on fifteen occasions, so that, if "air shots" had not been reckoned, he would have accomplished his task with just one stroke to spare.

As I said before, I have no knowledge of the Sorrento course, which probably bristles with difficulties, but my inclination would have been to back H. The only piece of evidence I have to go on comes back to me across the years from Aberdovey. Thither a good long while ago two public school masters used to bring a reading party of schoolboys in the summer holidays. One day every summer the party had a grand golf competition, and in this one of the masters used to take part, not because he wanted to, but out of pure good nature. It is true that he was not a complete beginner, because he had played in this competition several times. On the other hand, he certainly was not, in the words of the definition, "reasonably proficient in other sports", for I am gravely mistaken if he had ever played any kind of ball game in his life. Now, on the one occasion when I watched some part of his round, he took 210, and I would certainly have backed any good natural game-player, completely innocent of golf, to beat him. These remarks are rather insulting, perhaps, to H's game-playing talents, and I may be quite wrong, but I still think that if I might choose a good young cricketer or—better still, perhaps—racket player, he would get under that 200.

A good deal would depend on the "experimentee's" caddie, because, with eleven strokes allowed for each hole, the longest way round would constantly prove the shortest way home, and there would be much virtue in dodging the bunkers. I remember well in that far-off competition at Aberdovey that the player, making excellent progress by short stages, reached an admirable strategic position in front of the bunker guarding the first green in some five shots. We, who watched breathlessly, wondered whether he would go round, but no—he made a frontal attack and paid for his temerity, since he holed out, I think, in fifteen. An almost passionate humility is what the player needs, when he can afford to keep his score by an average of elevens. Perhaps there is here a lesson for us who are still apt to reckon by fours and ought to do so by fives.

I know of one case in point—a friend of mine whom I may, perhaps, have cited before. He enjoyed a liberal handicap,

with which he should have done well, but the terror of a
medal day was always too much for him, and his card, if it
did not positively float across the links of Hoylake in small
pieces, was quite unworthy of him. One day, however, a
very great man took him aside and told him to make out
beforehand, hole by hole, a score up to which he was to play.
It was to be conceived on humble lines, since he could afford
to be humble. At the first hole, for instance, he was to give
himself a six. That would enable him to steer a safe course far
away from that dreaded field into which the most respectable
persons have sliced many balls. The score proceeded in the
same manner all the way round. The component holes were
not in the least brilliant, but there was to be no major disaster,
and the total was such as should, with the handicap deducted,
give a good chance of victory. It had an excellent effect. Hole
after hole was played so precisely according to plan that on
one or two greens, when the player might have beaten the
prescribed figure, he putted with deliberate caution so as to
avoid doing so. If I remember the story rightly, he only let
himself go at the very last hole, where, contrary to his sailing
orders, he went for the carry over the cross-bunker with his
second, reached the green, got his four, and won the medal
in a blaze of triumph.

THE RE-BIRTH OF A GOLFER

There are few pleasanter stories and few which make one more bitterly envious than Hans Andersen's story of the Tinder Box. It will be remembered that the soldier had only to rub this box (which, I regret to say, he had stolen from an old witch) and three dogs instantly appeared before him, one with eyes as big as saucers, a second with eyes as big as mill wheels and a third whose eyes were positively of the size of towers. These dogs brought him money—copper, silver or gold—whenever he wanted it; they brought him the beautiful princess in her sleep, and they finally saved him from being executed when he richly deserved it, and frightened the King into giving him the princess as a bride.

They were, in short, the most invaluable animals, and they always set me thinking about the benevolent magician who will some day appear and grant me everything I wish. There is one wish which would, I believe, make us all happy, if we could have it granted. It is a very modest one, being no more than that we shall be allowed to begin all over again the learning of some pleasant art. There is bicycling, for instance, which to-day appears merely a tedious method of getting about when there is no car. Yet can anybody deny that there was a romantic thrill in his earliest wobbles on that despised instrument? I can remember wonderfully clearly my first beginnings, a blazing hot day in September on the lawn at home, an angelic and perspiring parent who held me and the bicycle, while we made curious zig-zags across the grass. And then the sensation of going unaided, and the first ride on the open highway! The Huntingdon road at Cambridge is not celebrated for its beauty; it is flat, straight and rather ugly; but when I think of that first bicycle—Somebody's *Grand Modèle de Luxe*—the road seems to me, in retrospect, to have been fringed by fairy trees and jewelled flowers.

I began golf so long ago and at such an immature age that
I can recall nothing about it, but it must have been delicious,
and I wish it could happen all over again. If one had the
strength of mind to do it, I believe it would be well worth
while to start again as a one-handed player and pant for the
day when one was given a twenty-four handicap. Or, perhaps,
left-handed would be better, because then one could laboriously transpose all the rules one had learnt and hold tight
with the right hand and loose with the left, and so on. No
doubt there would be disappointments in store, but one would
be getting slowly better instead of getting rather quickly
worse, and there are few sensations more enchanting than the
consciousness of improvement.

I have just had a letter from a golfer who began again
left-handed, and his experiences are rather interesting. He did
not do it deliberately from a spirit of adventure, but because,
owing to a rheumatic left shoulder, he could play no longer
in the ordinary way. So, after twenty years of right-handed
playing he became a humble novice, bought fresh clubs and
stood on the other side. "And do you know," he says, "it was
great fun." I am sure it must have been, and I envy him the
luxury of his feelings in that new blossoming. "I was a little
better, of course," he adds, "than when I started playing
right-handed, because I knew the importance of a steady head,
firm stance, and so on." That seems rather surprising. I will
not be so cynical as to say that these pieces of knowledge do
more harm than good, but I should not have expected them
to counterbalance the strangeness and topsy-turvey-dom of
being on the wrong side of the ball. Many years ago I amused
myself by cultivating a left-handed iron, and thought I did
attain to hitting a teed ball with a modest accuracy, I never
felt anything but horribly clumsy, a duffer with no touch and
no eye, who never would be anything but a duffer.

My correspondent was less humble, for he came to the
conclusion that, whereas his lowest handicap in his unregener-
ate days had been eight or nine, left-handed he was going to
be "a real tiger". Well, he wasn't; that is, in brief, the sad end
of the story. He soon found that he was "committing the
old mistakes in a very much accentuated form". He played
matches against "old, old men and middle-aged ladies", and

I rather gather that these despised persons would sometimes have beaten him, if it had not been for one circumstance; his shoulder was not so ill but that he retained the power of playing quite short strokes right-handed. Thus he could sometimes, when apparently *in extremis*, lay a pitch dead and dash the cup of victory from the old ladies' lips. The end of the story is not really sad, because in the last paragraph of his letter he tells me that his shoulder was suddenly cured, so that he could play right-handed once more. Moreover, he plays a little better for the discipline which he has undergone. Perhaps he carries one left-handed club in his bag and, when his ball lies apparently unplayable under a wall, he plays a brilliant shot with it and gives his enemy a shock just as he used to do to the old ladies.

To be able to play equally well from either side of the ball would be a wonderful thing. I am not thinking of that occasional ball wedged under a fence; I have just conceived the luminous idea that to this happy ambidextrous golfer the fear of slicing would be dead. If the wind blew hard on his back when he stood to the ball right-handed, he would just stand the other way and take a left-handed club and the slicy wind would become a hooky one: a friend and helper instead of a tyrannical foe. The prevailing wind at St. Andrews, in my experience at any rate, blows from left to right on the way out, and one is often so exhausted with fighting the slice and keeping out of the whins, that one has no energy left to revel in the hook on the inward half. To the ambidextrous golfer the round would be one long delicious orgy of hooking. With what freedom would he lash at his ball! What a splendid, virile, fearless creature he would be! When I get my tinder-box, here is another gift for me to wish for. Meanwhile, if I could find it, I would go out and practise with that old left-handed iron of mine; but, alas! I know it has been ruthlessly swept away to a jumble sale long since.

BLACK OR SILVER

The other day both my caddie and my irons reappeared after luncheon looking rather pale. On inquiry it appeared that the caddie had been trying to clean the irons, which had remained uncleaned since I visited America in 1922. No wonder the poor fellow looked wan; he had, by a prodigious display of energy, just got through the outer crust of dirt when a fellow-caddie had told him of my singular habits and bidden him desist. I felt thoroughly ashamed, the more especially as my play in the morning had justified his probable belief that his master had not used those irons for several years.

Once upon a time, to use unpolished clubs would have been unthinkable and, indeed, even now, after nine years of it, it sometimes gives me a shameful and slovenly feeling, as if I were to come down to breakfast unshaven. At the same time it is now recognised as a perfectly respectable thing, and hardly even eccentric, for the most illustrious persons do it. The first golfer of eminence whom I recollect playing with black clubs was Mr. Herbert Fowler. He was regarded for some years as an erratic genius and no one imitated him. Then—and I hope I am not defaming anyone—came Mr. Robert Harris and then several of the Americans, among them Mr. Bobby Jones, who, if he did not have his irons wholly black, at least forbade his caddie to clean the centres of them. After that the habit became for a while positively fashionable.

No doubt these distinguished persons had excellent reasons for their eccentricity. The statment is attributed to Young Tommy Morris that amateurs allow their eyes to be lured from the ball by the glitter of a polished head; that may have been one of the reasons, and there is much to be said for it. For myself I can assign no such easily defensible reason for my habit. It arose partly by chance, partly from pure laziness. When I was in America I found that the caddies considered it beneath the dignity of a free-born citizen to perform any such menial task. Therefore I paid the professional some fraction of a dollar to perform it, but I always had to leave that particular course before he had done so, and this offended my economical soul. Furthermore, on what may be called my home course I often dispense with a caddie, and I do not want the bother of cleaning my very muddy clubs after the round. Yet another reason is a decided popularity with the caddie, if I do have one, since he gets the orthodox tip and has less work to earn it. These are not, I admit, very good reasons, but there is one that is, namely, that clubs uncleaned will never wear out. If I live or play till ninety, I shall still be using, if I have a mind to it, the rather disreputable and ill-matched set of irons with which I now play my indifferent shots. The weight of a favourite iron can be slowly but surely altered in the course of years by cleaning, so that its owner wakes up suddenly one morning to find that he cannot "feel the head" because that head has grown "tinny" and emaciated.

I read somewhere the other day a remark of Duncan's that caddies must be watched with the eyes of a lynx when they clean clubs. They start, he said, with a new piece of sandpaper, on the heel of the iron and expend there the chief part of their elbow-grease, with the result that the heel becomes rapidly lightened and the balance of the club spoiled. I cannot say that I had noticed that subtle point for myself, but I am sure he is right, and about the more general altering of the weight there can be no doubt at all. Mr. Laidlay's famous putting cleek grew so thin with the years that at last he took to an ordinary aluminium putter. He then endeavoured to make us believe that this was the easier club to play with, but it was, I believe, only an artifice to cover up a tragedy. At the present moment I have taken once more to putting—it is, in my case, but a courtesy title—with a dear old cleek which I bought at Sandwich on the occasion of my first University match in 1895. It is still, in my eyes, a delicious club, but it has had to have some additional metal soldered to its back. If I had begun by keeping it unpolished, it might still be the original club which I bought from Ramsay Hunter and with which I used once to be able to putt almost well.

There are various other advantages of the non-cleaning policy that may be tentatively suggested. For instance, no one is likely to steal a club that appears superficially so grubby and unappetising. For that matter, I have—touching wood—never found anyone who wanted to steal my clubs or even to borrow them. Again, there is the rather disgraceful hope of picking up a stray half-crown or two by being a "flat-catcher". An unsuspecting stranger might well think that nobody could possibly hit the ball with so seedy an armoury of irons. Nevertheless, the owner of black clubs does now and then feel an almost passionate longing to have them cleaned, much as, I presume, the owner of a beard sometimes feels his fingers itch to shave it off, simply for the sake of novelty. Nor is this desire so foolish and capricious as it may appear, because novelty can improve our golf by giving us a new interest in the game. It is so easy for our minds as well as our bodies to get stale and bored.

I am sure I have quoted before the case of Mr. Guy Ellis, who, when in his brief and conquering prime, declared that he played three rounds of St. Andrews a day and used a different set of clubs for each round "because then it was impossible to get stale". I can cite other celebrated personages. When Sir Harold Gillies took to his monstrously high tee he played monstrously well for a while and could advance all sorts of reasons why the tee made it easier to swing the club. The reasons were doubtless unimpeachable, but it is my belief that they had mighty little to do with the matter, and that he played so well simply because his interest in the game was titillated. At the present moment he seems to have retired from the fray, but if he only discovers something else to amuse him, he will soon be beating everybody's head off again. May he discover that something quickly! Then there is Leo Diegel, who has an engagingly fantastic outlook on the game. He has a habit of suddenly having the head or the shaft of a wooden club painted another colour, or otherwise disguised in some such way, in order that the club, while unchanged in essentials, may seem to its owner to be a new one. Major Thorburn is another player who occurs to me. The leather grips of his wooden clubs come much farther down the shaft than is usual. This does not mean that he holds the clubs low down on the grip. His motive is, I believe, simply this: that the long grip makes the club look shorter, and he feels as if the shorter club would be easier to control.

Some people may think these antics of the great merely nonsensical, but, if they think so, they should suspect themselves of being too stolid and unimaginative. There is such a great deal of fun, and some profit as well, to be got out of the game which we called, when we were very young, "pretending". The trouble is that as we grow older we lose some of the power of playing it. A child can enjoy the game, even if it has to coach the grown-up in his part—thus: "Now I'll hide under the table, and then you say, 'I wonder where that naughty, tiresome little girl can have got to'." When the poor, stupid grown-up has said his first sentence like a parrot, he is taught his next one, and so the game goes on in instalments. When we are old we cannot rise to such heights of pretending; but still, if we are not too self-conscious, we never wholly lose the knack of it and can recapture more of it by deliberate effort. So, if anybody sees me playing with beautifully burnished irons, he need not think that I have succeeded to a large estate and bought some new ones; I shall only be pretending that I have acquired a wonderful new numbered set from America and that I am going to hit the ball with the crisp click of a shutting knife for ever more.

THE COLONEL AND THE RABBIT

A gentleman of my acquaintance has just written me a letter which provides—and perhaps he little knows how grateful I am to him—a theme for a golfing discourse. He has, in his own picturesque language, "exchanged the toga of the proconsul for the grey flannel trousers of the rabbit". In other words, he has come home with nothing much to do, and has been amusing himself by playing in a number of old boy and other similar golfing competitions. These "orgies" (I really do not know why he calls them that) usually culminate in foursomes against Bogey. This is where his complaint begins. It would obviously be an impertinence for me to paraphrase or abbreviate a proconsul. Moreover, it will save me some trouble not to do so, and he writes in a highly entertaining manner. So here he is in his own words, and let us pay him the proper tribute of a new paragraph:

"I have always understood," he says, "that Bogey was an elderly and methodical Colonel of the age which, nowadays when we are all young, is euphemistically called middle. After the State has dispensed with his services he has applied to the game of golf that meticulous accuracy and rigorous routine which had made him the terror of barrack square and orderly room alike. As a consequence, with a swing short and snappy like his old word of command, he could be trusted to propel the ball with any implement down the fairway to any distance up to a maximum, reasonable but somewhat curtailed. Once on the green he holed in two putts, never more, never less. But my experience over a variety of courses has shown me how false these ideas are. If Bogey is indeed a Lieutenant-Colonel, he can be no rheumatic and livery ex-commandant of a regiment, but must be a young and lissom Captain with a double brevet. Holes of well over 400 yards are to him, as the primrose was to Peter Bell, a four and nothing more. It seems to me that Colonel Bogey has forgotten the dignity and restraint due to his rank and has taken in defiance of military discipline to associating on terms of dangerous equality with Captain Par."

My correspondent finds this particularly exasperating because he himself, when, as will happen occasionally, he meets the ball with the full face of the club, can hit it a good deal farther than can most of his military friends. Nevertheless, there are certain holes which Colonel Bogey does in four, and yet he cannot reach them in two of his best shots. Consequently, he has been besieging committees with requests for information, and the committees have given him but little satisfaction. Some of them gave him white bread in the answer that "it is necessary to have a test whereby members may be assessed to scratch"; some gave him brown bread—"that it would be ridiculous to have a Bogey competition won by a score of eight up"; some did not even give him plum cake, but contemptuously drummed him out of town. With these replies he is discontented. He thinks that Par is always available for those who want to be tested, and, further, that "if out of eighty members playing under handicap one of them at least cannot register a substantial advantage over an accurate but elderly Colonel playing from scratch, the local system of handicapping must be flattering." Therefore he writes to me, as he says, for enlightenment, but, as I imagine, rather for sympathy.

I suspect my correspondent of wanting to pull the joint and several legs of those committees, as also of myself. Presuming, however, that he is not so disrespectful, then I think that the answer to him is tolerably clear. An insufficient knowledge of history has misled him as to the real character of Bogey. I have always been taught that what we now call Bogey was first instituted at Coventry; that it was what may vaguely be termed a scratch score for the course, computed for the purpose of a then novel competition, and that it was originally known as the "ground score" of the course. Next someone called it Bogey because of the then popular song (which I shall be delighted to whistle to my correspondent), "The Bogey Man." Finally, some wag at a Service golf club, I think Haslar, added the "Colonel". If this be so, the legend about

Bogey being short and elderly grew up on account of his name
and has no real historical foundation. At Aberdovey, in about
1892 (as I am sure I have stated before), we played foursomes
against Colonel Bogey and Professor Goblin, but we had no
earthly right to confer that professorship—also a symbol of
elderliness and shortness. In the Ordnance, a corps in which
I had the honour of serving during the War, there was long
ago a number of civilian potentates. Perhaps they were called
"commissaries", perhaps—for I have forgotten—by some
even more splendid title. At any rate, a change was made, and
these personages went to bed one night as civilians and woke
up next morning as lieutenant-colonels. As there chanced to
be forty of them, they were known as the forty thieves: so, at
least, I used to be told, though I accept no responsibility for
the story. I merely tell it to show what kind of a colonel Bogey
was and is.

Now, if I am right, the original Bogey was just a sound,
average, scratch golfer, of no particular age, playing his game.
The colonel is a mere gloss, and my friend has no right to
complain because now and again a scratch player can reach
in two shots some hole that he himself cannot. May I add this
at the risk of affronting him? I have always understood that
Bogey is supposed to hole in four strokes only those holes
that he can reach with an iron or spoon for his second shot;
when he needs two full wooden-club shots he takes five to
the hole. In that respect he is clearly a player whose game has
its limitations; he is not a great one, but there is no justification
for accusing him of a positively senile shortness.

There is, to my mind, a much more justifiable complaint
against Bogey. While he is alleged to maintain, and does
maintain, taking the round as a whole, a deadly monotony
of form, his game varies in an almost capricious manner from
hole to hole. At one hole of 410 yards or so he takes four, at
another of precisely the same length he takes five. At the
one-shot holes he is even less to be depended upon; sometimes
he takes three and sometimes four, and no one knows how
he drops that one stroke, though, presumably, it is never on
the putting green. Of course, he must be made to drop these
occasional strokes or he would be much better than a scratch
player. The poor committeemen, that my friend wants to kill,

really cannot be blamed for that; but when people plume themselves, as they sometimes do, on beating Bogey at a particular hole, they ought to remember that he is much easier to beat at some holes than others.

If my friend really wants to send round the fiery cross and start some kind of crusade against poor old Bogey, I have still another point to suggest to him. Bogey originally provided a good medium for a pleasant easy-going competition without the worst agonies of medal play. That is his proper function, and it should not be extended, but some golfers regard him so firmly as setting up a standard that, as it seems to me, they lose all understanding of the game of golf. Take, for example, the sort of hole that is all too common. It is just too long to be reached by two good shots, but it can be reached by three exceedingly moderate ones, in the playing of which there is neither interest nor excitement. Somebody points out that by putting the tee forward a little the hole can be vastly improved, since it would then be reachable in two good and entertaining shots. Thereupon the reformer is met with a remark of this sort: "Yes, it might be a good hole, but I don't think we could change it. You see, it's a Bogey five hole." Could imbecility go farther? I hardly think so, and yet that is a remark I have often heard made by otherwise sane persons. If it is better to have a thoroughly dull, bad hole which is "a Bogey five" rather than a testing and amusing one, which this legendary being can do in four, then what is the good of anything? I am sure I don't know, but perhaps my friend who is studying this question can discover.

A PROPHET IN THE WILDERNESS

Towards the end of the year we remember one another with a shock and try to atone for twelve months of forgetfulness by hearty, contrite letters. It is therefore appropriate that this season should bring me from distant climes not so much a letter as an encyclopaedia on the subject of golf. Its author— and I love him for writing—was but a year ago struggling for a place in one of the University sides. Today he is taking his first step in the country's service, miles from any of his kind, in one of the "outposts of Empire".

He has been provident enough not to leave his clubs behind and he describes himself in his few moments of leisure practising the perfect swing before, as he says, a larger gallery of black men than ever he had of white ones. He is in the bush and his normal occupation is that of fighting locusts. Fortunately this involves the burning of long grass, so that here and there is a place where he can set himself a lonely examination in the making of strokes. There is one shot in particular "of the kind," he says, "which you have, I believe, described as exhilarating." I am sure I have done so—all too often —but still, it is flattering of him to remember it and perhaps once upon a time the epithet was not ill chosen. It seems that there is a large rock with a tiny patch of turf on the top of it, whence there is a carry of nearly 200 yards across grass and "guinea corn", whatever that may be, to a stony hill over the way. Here is a pleasant picture, which some day his biographers may like to recall: the young proconsul, "high in the stainless eminence of air" upon his rock, lashing ball after ball. There was—here observe the earnest student of the game—"a slight left-hand wind", and "the ball was going off very sweetly, so that everybody was pleased". His skill will gain him some local title of honour. The people of Kukuana, if I remember rightly, christened Sir Henry Curtis Incubu the

Elephant, for his strength. My friend will doubtless be named the Tiger.

This description of the writer's doings occupies but a small part of his letter. The greater part of it is taken up with his views on the game, excogitated in solitude. One of these at least strikes me as distinctly original. He declares that those who write primers of instruction do not sufficiently take into account the fact that "there are two classes of golfers, the good and the bad". This rather bald statement he amplifies by defining the bad not as those who cannot now hit the ball but as those who never will be able to do so, just because they have no "eye", no natural style, and, in short, no instinct for hitting any sort of ball or playing any sort of game. It is vain to lay down the same rules, "beyond the very basic principles," for these two classes. The "good", he thinks, may be allowed a certain licence to trust in their natural instinct and sense of style or touch, but with the poor "bad" it is otherwise; "if the incurable class want to play well enough to give themselves the satisfaction of improving, they must keep to the most rigid letter of the law."

The particular piece of advice which moved my friend to make this statement is that of Mr. Bobby Jones, who has said that in putting the player should allow himself some little movement of the body. That, he thinks, is all very well for the "good" player who may move a little if he wants to, because thus "he will be giving his touch full scope"; the "bad" is only increasing for himself the number of possible pitfalls, and "has not got the bodily equipment to avoid them." There seems to me one answer to this—namely, that the "bodily equipment" of the bad player unfits him nearly as much to keep rules as to break them. It may be true enough that if he is told to move he will lurch. Is it not also true that if he is told to stand still he will stand at attention in such a frozen stillness that he will be incapable of hitting the ball? I have not thought deeply on this subject in the intervals of fighting locusts, and my friend may very well be right, but I cannot help thinking that, rules or no rules, it is heads the good player wins and tails the bad player loses.

Another of my correspondent's views—I have missed out

one or two—seems to me of the soundest, and it is the more remarkable as coming from the younger generation. He says that too many of his contemporaries have wholly forgotten the possibilities of the half or the spared shot. Consequently "we have the unedifying spectacle of people who ought to know better hitting themselves sick with mashie-niblicks (only they prefer to call them No. 7's) up to a distance of 150 yards, and often with nothing but grass between themselves and the hole." To these observations many elder golfers will wish to reply, as Sam Weller did to the gentleman in light blue with leaden buttons: "Your health, Sir. I like your conwersation much, I think it's wery pretty." And what a splendid chance my correspondent has of putting this admirable view into practice! The great difficulty about half-shots is that we seldom have the courage to play them in a real match. We go out alone and practise them both virtuously and successfully; but when there is an adversary of flesh and blood we hesitate and fall back on that which comes more easily to the average person, the full slog with the lofted club. But my poor friend—I pity as well as envy him—cannot play a real game, and so can practise and practise away from his rock, till he has really "grooved" that half-shot and has no temptation towards his mashie-niblick. I like to picture him doing so, while his feudal gallery make pyrotechnic noises. Meanwhile I send him belatedly all good wishes for the New Year, and may he soon come home to display the fruits of his labours by winning a championship.

THE NECESSARIES

A recent case in the Law Courts has produced a learned, comprehensive, and far from dry-as-dust judgment on the garments which are so necessary to a lady as to render her husband liable to pay for them. There has not yet been a case as to what are necessaries among golf clubs, but there well may be one in time. If it be tried by a cricketing or lawn-tennis playing Judge counsel for the plaintiff club-maker will be hard put to it to persuade the Court that a minimum of eight numbered irons is essential to a lady in order that she may not disgrace her husband on the links. Expert witnesses will be cross-examined as to whether, even if the husband had £5,000 a year, the wife could not do perfectly well without a spade mashie. If he barely pays supertax and she can use a spoon, a No. 1 iron will be denounced as an extravagance. Moreover, if the husband, though reasonably prosperous, likes to play his golf modestly with a maid-of-all-work iron, which he deliberately keeps black and rusty, it may be held that the wife must conform to his standard. The whole question bristles with difficulties, and we may imagine irons Nos. 2 and 3 being handed up to the learned Judge, who, after putting on his spectacles, declares, amid roars of laughter, that as far as he can see they might just as well be marked Tweedledum and Tweedledee.

If he did say so he might not be so absurdly wrong, as the following simple narrative will show. The other day, playing in a match on the New Course at Addington, I came in the second round to the ninth hole. I said to my caddie that I had made a respectable shot there in the morning with No. 3 iron and so would take it again. "I beg your pardon, Sir," he answered with extreme politeness, "but it was No. 2." We argued a little, but he was so positive that I gave in, merely asserting that I had *thought* I was using No. 3. My ensuing shot with No. 2 went far to prove him right since, far from going past the hole, I was a number of yards short of it. We went along with no further arguments till we came to the seventeenth, also a one-shot hole. Here, being quite certain as to what club I had taken in the morning, I demanded No. 2. This time he did not contradict me, but, again in a most soothing and urbane tone, said: "I think, Sir, No. 3 would do." The match was in a critical state; that green is demoniacally narrow; and confidence was the one essential thing, and he was a good and keen caddie. So without looking at the head I took the club he gave me and banged away. It was a very good shot, though I say it; everything was rosy and golden; the club went straight back into the bag and the putter came out in its place, but I am not now quite sure whether I played the stroke with No. 2 or No. 3 and whether that trusty caddie did not deceive me in my own interests.

That is perhaps from my point of view rather a humiliating story, and I tell it from no egotistical motives but merely as an illustration of the qualities of modern club-making. It shows how skilful were those (I wish I could give them a little puff) who blended two admirable steel shafts with two admirable heads that differed ever so slightly only in point of loft. Obviously the two clubs felt almost exactly alike in the hand, and they still do so now that I am on my guard; for all I know No. 1 and No. 4 might deceive me if I waggled them with my eyes shut. It is a thing that never could have happened with my dear old discarded and unnumbered ones, which had been picked up casually one at a time.

This may appear a sad, even a disgraceful admission, but when once a man has given up a coat and taken to a jersey or a jerkin he is capable of anything and dead to all sense of shame. Apologies for such modernity would be vain. I am, however, still sufficiently a Tory not to call my niblick No. 8 and to wonder whether all the different numbers are quite necessary. If ever I take them all out at once several of them come home at the end of the day as clean as when they set out. This shows, I suppose, that there is something seriously amiss with their owner's method, and Heaven knows there may be many things. My own belief is that nobody who was brought up in older ways will ever be able to use quite so many clubs as do the moderns. Observe this fortunate modern player. Once he has, after diving head foremost into his capacious bag, got his right number, his troubles appear to be at an end. There is no question of what sort of stroke to play; he just takes up his one stance and performs his own swing, with, I am bound to admit, excellent results. This beautiful simplicity and uniformity are not for his elders. With them there comes a point when they ask their caddie in their queer, archaic language whether it is a wrist shot. When their ball is at a certain distance from the pin their right foot will edge forward to a more open stance, the hands will creep a little lower down the grip; they positively want to hit the ball with a much curtailed follow through, because Mr. Laidlay, one of their queer old gods, said that when you swung an iron you went wrong. They are so odd that to them there seems something indecent and almost blasphemous in taking a full swing so near the green and that—gracious heavens!—with a mashie niblick, which will send the ball uncharted miles up into the air. They will try to play their half shots which they used to be told were the sure hall-mark of a golfer. I do not say they do it noticeably well or that they get as near the hole as do their juniors. I am only trying to make excuses for their not being able to find a use for all that lovely shiny phalanx of clubs.

If I could imagine myself a judge trying the hypothetical case suggested, I should ungallantly inquire how long the lady had been playing golf. If it were a good long time and she wanted something between her No. 3 and her mashie I should say with Best, C. J., in the case of Mr. Benedict, "The Court cannot enter into these little delicacies." If she were quite young I should have reluctantly to allow her a No. 4. My dear old friend, Smith's Leading Cases, has incidentally some remarks on lunatics' necessaries, but they presumably have no application.

ON NEVER SAYING DIE

A little while ago several golfers were in danger of losing their amateur status in that they were trying to teach golf for reward. There is a friend of mine, an admirable player, who has an elbow. He has submitted it to the most rigorous discipline, but every now and again, and that always through sheer "cussedness" on important occasions, it insists on flying into the air at the top of his swing. After a tragic morning round he offered a handsome fee—quite a large number of pounds—to any one who could cure him, and there were many eager to earn it. The links were dotted with physicians. Some stood close to the patient and shut one eye in a knowing manner; others stood afar off, thinking thus to gain a more comprehensive view and watched that elbow, trying to discover at what precise moment sinfulness entered into it. There were practically-minded persons who told him to dig himself violently in the ribs at the beginning of the swing. More subtle thinkers professed to see that the poor elbow had no criminal instincts, but was forced into evil courses by that arch-crook, the body. My own amateur conscience is clear, for, having an elbow myself, I said that there was nothing for it but church-yard mould, and made no attempt to gain the reward. The end of the story cannot be told here. The patient, buoyed up by various prescriptions, went out to play nine holes. At the end of the nine his wife wanted him to come home, but he said, briefly, that he would find his own way back, and was last seen heading for the tenth green after a magnificent tee shot.

There is a temptation here to embark on a treatise about elbows. I know a picture in an old Scottish text-book, much older than that in the *Badminton*, showing a billycock-hatted gentleman at the top of his swing, with his right elbow waving high above his billycock. How much additional suffering it must have caused in a suffering world! The Americans have invented a cure in the shape of a strap and buckle, which keep the elbows together. I could not afford enough dollars, but I did once truss my elbows together by means of an old tie, and thus manacled performed prodigies of skill in a lonely meadow. My friend might do worse than try this plan, but, after all, to be captain of one's elbow is a small thing; it is a great thing to be captain of one's soul and, whatever the end of his story, he is an example of the indomitable spirit of golfers.

"You can trick them and mock them with all the implements of fate—lead them on only to betray them, obsess them with hopeless dreams, punish them with senseless accidents, and harass them with wretched fears. You can buffet them, bait them, enrage them—load upon them all evils and follies in this vale of obstruction and tears. But, even at that, there is yet one thing that you cannot do. You can never make them, under any provocation, say die."

The author of *The Midnight Bell* did not write those inspiring words primarily of golfers, but of the whole race of men. I am not even sure whether he plays golf, but if he does not he has been granted, without his knowing it, the power of looking deep into their souls, for nothing truer was ever written about them. "Mock them with all the implements of fate"! Yes, indeed, think of all that steel shafts were going to do for us and yet our handicaps are still on the rise. "Hopeless dreams and senseless accidents"! Was I not going to win that medal if at the very first hole my ball had not kicked horribly, inexplicably, contrary to the laws of God and man, into the bunker? "Wretched fears"! Am I not so much afraid of going off at half-cock upon the green that I cannot force myself to take my putter back, but stand there transfixed and impotent? And yet have I not just returned from practising in a muddy hayfield, where I lost several balls and grew unpleasantly warm, and do I not believe that I have found out a brand-new something? An hour since I was, as a golfer, extinct; now for the hundredth time I have come to life again.

These remarks are in the first person, but they need not have been, for they are true of all the bravest, stupidest race in the world, the unconvincible, inextinguishable race of golfers. Only a little while ago I was playing in a tournament together with a very good golfer who thinks he is getting too old. He was tired out, for he had overplayed and overworked himself for other people's benefit; he almost wanted to be beaten, and when he was beaten he said that all he longed for was to put away his clubs and turn to his guns. That was on the Tuesday night. On Wednesday his sentiments remained apparently the same, and this perfervid being actually rested. On Thursday there was a change; after a long day's watching he sneaked out on to the lawn with a driver and some soft balls; he teed them carefully on a marked line, so as to see whether he was hitting "from the inside out", and slogged them to the end of the lawn tennis court and back over the path and into the flower beds. On the Friday he was busy practising with hard balls and felt once more as if he could stand up and follow through like an American. For the Saturday he had engaged to play in a four-ball match over 36 holes. He said he thought he could beat those two and it would be rather fun to try. I hope he succeeded, but it does not matter. They could never make him say die.

It has been written, I think by Mr. Wells, that once a man in his heart acknowledges another as his superior the game is up. That can surely not be true of golfers, for comparatively few of us think that we are as good as Mr. Bobby Jones, and yet we go flogging, analysing, discovering on. The nearest approach to that blissful belief is to be found presumably among professionals, who in handicap competitions with amateurs are all placed on the same mark (plus six or plus four), with no unkind discriminations made between them. That must be very soothing, and yet they might not remain so pleased with the system if they had to play ordinary half-crown matches under it. To us poor amateurs, handicapping committees, for all that they are often too indulgent to human weaknesses, are yet sad disturbers of our vanity. For all of us there is a moment when we come to the parting of the ways and must decide either to accept other people's estimate of us or never again to play in a monthly medal. And there is yet one further stage in which we never play a match, but only go out practising and lose ourselves in beautiful futile dreams from which there is no rude awakening.

THE LINKS OF EIDERDOWN

Given exactly the right conditions, there are few pleasanter things than a day in bed. We must not be rank imposters; we must be just ill enough to be sure that we shall be nearly well next day or, indeed, quite well so long as we have not to come down to breakfast. We must feel equal not to gross roast beef but to a whiting sympathetically eating its own tail and to a rice pudding, not forgetting the brown sugar. Tobacco, though sparingly indulged in, must not take on the flavour of hay, and though wholly incapable of answering a newly arrived letter, we must be well able to read an old book.

It is best, if possible, to feel some warning symptoms the night before, so that we may be assured that it would be very unwise to get up next morning. Thus we have the joys both of anticipation and of fruition. That such joys are selfish it cannot be denied. The telephone bell rings in the distance and we cannot answer it. The bell rings for luncheon, and there are sounds of scurrying feet as of those late in washing; we are taking a little holiday in that respect and our lunch comes up on a tray. With what heavenly malice do we hear a strange motor-car crunching the gravel under the window. Callers—ha, ha! The new neighbours—ho, ho! We shall be told later that they proved to be very agreeable people and we are perfectly ready to take it on trust. With a last thought of them sitting ranged round the drawing-room, we drift away into a beautiful half-way house between sleep and waking without fearing any of the misery that ensues if we do the same thing in a chair. We shall come to ourselves as bright as a button and ready for another go of *David Copperfield*.

This was my admirable choice last week, and I was so drowsily happy that I found even Agnes "pointing upward" not unendurable. Only one thing disturbed my serenity. In

my warped mind's eye I continually saw golf holes designed on
the "land of counterpane" before me. It is not an uninteresting
one, this links of eiderdown, and is laid out on what an
ingratiating prospectus would call fine, undulating country.
Moreover, by undulating himself in bed the patient can in a
moment change the contour of his course. In the ordinary
way there is a broad hog's-back ridge extending down the
middle of the course. It is doubtless possible to use it in several
ways, but I always saw a long plain hole running nearly the
whole length of it, slightly downhill with a fall to perdition
on either side for the slicer or the hooker. It seemed to me, if
I remembered the number aright, rather like the 13th hole at
Liphook. There were no bunkers on it of any kind; no
"lighthouses", as the more ferocious of architects scornfully
term them, to guide the eye of the tiger and make superfluously
wretched the rabbit's life; nothing but a wide expanse on
which it would clearly be very difficult to judge distance.

When my eyes dropped to either side of this ridge I felt that
I was in another country. Was I at Formby or Birkdale, or
perhaps at the 6th hole at Prince's, Sandwich? Here, at any
rate, was one of the holes that run along a narrow valley with
slopes on either hand—on one side, to be precise, the patient's
leg, and on the other the outside edge of the eiderdown. I
have always had rather a romantic affection for such holes. I
have heard with pain from those same "highbrow" architects
that they are not really good holes, because the mere fact of
the banks (which will kick the ball back to the middle) give
the player confidence, whereas the architect's duty is to make
him hesitating and uncomfortable. I began to think that these
irritating views were right; the valley might be narrow, but I
felt as if I could drive straight down it, whereas when I looked
at the ridge I did not feel nearly so happy.

There were other holes on the course, but they were hardly
so satisfactory. There was, to be sure, a big, blind tee shot, to
a one-shot hole as I imagined it, over a comparatively noble
hill, made by my toes, but somehow it lacked subtlety; and
when by a swift piece of engineering I moved the hill to see
what the green was like on the far side, it proved flat and
featureless. By separating and then adroitly manipulating my
two sets of toes it was possible to make a crater green, with

visions of the ball running round the side wall and back wall to lie dead at least for an unmerited three. That brought back sentimental memories. I knew a beloved course once that had three such greens running, and many years ago I had three threes running there and won a medal thereby. Still, the sweetness of such threes has a cloying quality. No doubt it is all for the best in the most testing of all possible worlds that there should be no more greens like that nowadays.

To roll over on my side had a disappointing effect on the links. In fact it was obviously not a links any longer, but a mere course: one of those courses on downland which I have the misfortune to dislike, with long, steep slopes, equally tedious to play up or down, and too often adorned with "gun-platform" greens. When tea came, however, the course took on a new aspect, for the tea-tray was on a bed table and the bed table had four legs. The course was now one cut out of a wood, on which the architect had wisely allowed a solitary sentinel tree or two to remain standing in the middle of the fairway. The valley holes instantly became far more interesting, for each of them had one tree, acting in some sort as a Principal's Nose, for the tee shot, and another, like that capital tree at the first hole at Frilford, bang in front of the green. I spent some time trying to resolve on which side of those trees to go. At one hole it seemed best to try the right-hand line, because if I went to the left I might hook on to the floor, which was clearly out of bounds. At the other hole an exactly converse policy was indicated, but even with the banks to help me the shot was far from easy.

Now I am, as Mr. Littimer would say, "tolerably well" again, and *David Copperfield* is finished. I have no reasonable pretext for not getting up for breakfast, and indeed it is rumoured that there are to be sausages tomorrow morning. The links of eiderdown are fast becoming of the fabric of a dream. I have tried to fix the holes before they elude the frantic clutches of memory and fade away into one another.

CROWD AND URGENCY

We cannot have a great occasion without a crowd. To see and hear in comfort is a desire that grows upon us with age and laziness, but comfort and excitement, though they may live together, can never be true friends. The perfection of poignancy can only be enjoyed by the uncomfortable, and the longing to wave the hat in the air in an ecstasy of triumph is never so keenly felt as when the arms are firmly pinned to the side by the pressure of our next-door neighbours. We may and very likely do hate those neighbours, but they contribute to our excitement for all that, and we feel their thrills not only physically but mentally. The blocked road, the railway carriage with ten people standing in it, the fighting a way to our seats—these are all exquisitely uncomfortable but they add an exquisite flavour to our sensations. Once we grow frightened of them, as I admit I have done, the game is up.

Of the sights enjoyed in youth it is the excitement of the crowd that survives when the spectacle itself has almost wholly vanished from the memory. In 1887 I was taken to see Queen Victoria's Jubilee procession. Save for a general feeling of the unspeakable glory of the Life Guards all has gone. Even the tiny bowing figure in the carriage, the very heart and centre of all that magnificence, has grown very dim. But what remains distinctly is the staying the night before in Kensington, the thrill of early breakfast, the driving as far as the four-wheeler was allowed, and then the walking through yellow sanded streets already lined with people, till the appointed eyrie was reached. That was the crowded hour, there was the glorious life.

I am writing these words soon after watching, in the contemptible luxury of a garden on the river, the University Boat Race. If ever there was an example of the value of crowd and urgency it is this festival. It was a fine sunny day, but with a biting east wind. A million people were there to see, and of those all but the tiniest proportion were at least as ignorant as I am of the art of rowing and had no reason, but a purely artificial partisanship, to care who won. They stood in serried ranks for some hours, they saw the boats for little more than a moment, and for most of the race only the possibility that Cambridge might catch a second crab in that poppling water could avert the inevitable end. That does not sound a particularly enthralling entertainment and yet I have no doubt that those million onlookers found it good fun, and it was good fun.

As far as the race itself was concerned it was all too soon over. There came the cry of "Here they are" from those perched on a roof nearby, and then the flash of the oars after Hammersmith Bridge, the light blue in front and sparkling cheerfully in the sunlight. For a minute or two we saw the boats and the crowd of following steamers; then they were hidden from us by Chiswick Eyot. The great waves of the steamers surged and splashed against our guardian wall, and after that the river returned once more to comparative emptiness and placidity, the spectators began to disperse, and there was nothing for it but to return indoors to a fire and listen on the wireless to Cambridge—it was Cambridge and that was something—drawing comfortably away to victory.

Nevertheless, I repeat it was uncommonly good fun. There was the packing of the sandwich basket, the settling down to the drive, the wondering whether we should be blockaded as we drew near to Hammersmith, the sight of more and more people obviously making for the river, bent on a common enterprise. It was Hazlitt on the Bath coach going to see the fight at Newbury all over again; on a rather mild scale admittedly, but much can be done by a little imagination. Just because it was a great occasion, the hours of waiting assumed an agreeable tenseness and things ordinarily dull took on a new and vivid interest. We called to each other to look at a procession of steamers, much as we should once have exclaimed at a traction engine thundering down the lane; we felt sorry for the swans rocking in their wash. We watched the spectators accumulating ever more thickly on the Surrey shore and wondered maliciously whether the tide would rise high enough to wet their toes. In short we made the very most of a very little.

Supposing—a singularly futile but pleasing speculation—that we were the Emperor in Hans Andersen's story of "The Emperor's New Clothes". If we could decree anything we had a mind to, we might be tempted to order the Boat Race to be rowed for our private and imperial benefit. Even as William Rufus laid waste the New Forest for his hunting, the banks and the bridges should be cleared of onlookers; all the houses along the river must keep their blinds down and we should follow the race sitting under a canopy in a solitary launch blazing with gold. It is a thoroughly disgraceful project and would bring its own reward. We should be proved very stupid and unfit for our position, for the entertainment would fall as flat as a pancake and the oarsmen would scarcely trouble to row, except for the fear of having their heads cut off. And so it would be if any of our other selfish day-dreams could come to pass. A test match, played on the best wicket in the world within our own park palings would lapse into a mere exhibition of skill. Perhaps the most thrilling of all moments in any contest is that of the sudden hush that precedes it, but it would be as nothing if it were only the silence of absent thousands. We might as well hope to get the greatest of all orators to make a speech to us in an empty room as to enjoy a match without the barbarous yells of triumph that greet the fall of a wicket. Without the crowd there can be no urgency.

I, whose business it has been to watch golf, have superficially as good a reason to hate the crowd as have most people. At other games it is kept within bounds but the golf crowd is fluid and pours over the field of play. By much shouting and stewarding and roping it is to some extent restrained, but ever and anon it breaks through and runs wildly and tumultuously. It prevents me from seeing what I want to see, and yet, on purely selfish grounds, I would not be without it, for it can be the most dramatic of all the crowds in the world. The great black ring six deep round the putting green, the silence unbroken save by the curlews calling overhead, is a sight infinitely and eternally exciting. In any golfing scene that I remember over the years the crowd plays its part.

How often have I seen—how often, alas! have I described?—John Ball starting down the first hole in a great match with a rose in his button hole, with the trampling and the hum of the prayerful Hoylake crowd behind him, held back by the blue-jerseyed fishermen manning the rope. To ancient hero-worshippers of my generation there never was and never can be again so moving a spectacle as that. But others, second only to it, come back. There is Bobby Jones winning the Open Championship at St. Andrews. His ball lies in the hollow before the home green, called the Valley of Sin. The crowd are halted solid behind him. The moment he has played his shot and scrambled up the bank, the crowd rush up irresistibly behind him and halt again, making a black fringe round the green.He taps in his winning putt and the next moment there is no inch of green to be seen, nothing but a swirling mob, with Bobby in the middle, perched on adoring shoulders and his putter, "Calamity Jane", held in precarious safety over his head.

Even more tremendous, in point of sheer numbers, is the scene of our lone victory in the Walker Cup, when all but one match is finished, and the individual crowds that have been watching the others come streaming over the burn, with divisions melting into corps, and corps into one great army, converging on the cockpit of the home green. Better a thousand times to have been crushed and buffeted, and to have seen little but "the 'oofs and the 'orses" than to have missed so splendidly terrifying a spectacle. To-day at St. Andrews we who watch are herded to the side-lines among the whins. It has to be for the sake of the players and we ourselves see far more than we used to do, if at longer range, but something of the old drama has departed.

THE EVENING ROUND

A correspondent has written to me saying that the time has surely come for me to dilate upon golf after tea. He even goes so far as to say that I ought to do it every year, and here, being painfully conscious of my own bad habits, I thought at first that I detected a rather bitter irony. On re-reading his letter I came to the conclusion that he meant kindly; the irony is to be found in the circumstance, which he did not know, that I am not allowed to play golf even before tea.

The supreme moment can only come once a year, and this year I have missed it. For certain people it always comes on the same day, the Saturday of a week-end at Worlington. Then when the serious business of the day is over we sally forth with one club apiece. No doubt other and happier people did so last Saturday, but I had gone home snuffling and sneezing to bed, and that particular moment cannot be recaptured till another whole year has passed. Even as I write, some time after tea, there is plenty of light in the garden, light for putting and pitching, light even for what I am pleased to call driving, but it may not be.

The case, it may be said, is not a very hard one; the time of the first green mist on the hedges, of the first cuckoo that is not a mischievous little boy, has not yet come; there are plenty of evenings ahead. Yet the maddening part of golf is that the only time we feel a real longing to play it is when we cannot do so. In the morning I was allowed out for a little walk in the fresh air. I was exceedingly well wrapped up, and felt like Uncle Joseph in the coat of marten's fur and the health boots prescribed by Sir Faraday Bond. All Nature seemed determined to emphasise my lamentable state. In a little wood a missel-thrush sang loudly and triumphantly, and if ever a thrush sang "Golf after tea" that was the identical bird.

Through the wood there runs a wide, grassy glade. It was all flecked with sunshine and had in it just a suspicion of a "dog leg" bend to the right, that kept calling and calling in my ears for a shot with a little drift in it. I plodded to the end of it—the prescribed limit of my walk—and turned; there was an equally fascinating bend to the left, and it positively shouted, "Now for a little hook!" Outside the wood lay a meadow, bathed in light, close-cropped and inviting, with not so much as a single intrusive cow in it. All the new styles that I had thought of as I lay in my bed came welling up simultaneously in my mind and I could not try a single one of them, because it would never do to get "overheated." I was assured that I should be able to do it another day, but I did not want to do it another day; I may never want to do it on any other day, but I did so dreadfully want to have just one shot then.

There is something magical about the first rounds of Spring, so that we remember some of them long, long after we have played them, not on account of any petty personal triumphs or disasters, but from the pure joy of being alive, club in hand. There was one Easter half at school, when the sun was so hot and the ground was so dry that I lay and basked on the grass between my shots. I can see the particular spot now, just after turning away from the river and the terrific short hole with the solitary willow behind the green. There was another round at Sandwich, a first round on that noble course before a first University match. There was no lying on the grass that time, but a rush straight from the station to the club-house, and a race round the course in a blue serge suit to beat the fading daylight. Yet the same kind of ecstatic glory hangs round the memories of both rounds; I know that in the first of them my driver had a brown head, and in the second a yellow one, or perhaps, since the occasion was so romantic, I should say, of palest gold.

By way of encouraging in myself this maudlin state of mind I have been looking in an ancient diary to see which day of the year, something over thirty years ago, saw the first evening round. As a rule it was, year in and year out, within a day or two of this very Saturday, March 9th, but in one year it came much earlier. On one 25th of February I find recorded a tremendous display of energy; first of all a thirty-six-hole single, won at the very last hole, and then "Played a fourteen-hole match afterwards, which lost." Since no margin is given I think it may safely be stated that it was lost by a good many holes. What time of the morning we started and why we did it I cannot state; indeed if I did not know myself to have kept that diary with remarkable honesty I should not believe in the entry any more than I believe in those gentlemen who are incapable of deception and write to the newspapers to say that they have heard the cuckoo in February.

The time of third rounds is over and will not come back. It is pitch-dark outside my window now, but the daylight will come back and perhaps, if it is very warm and sunshiny, I shall be let out, without that confounded muffler, for just one spring shot with my springy driver. I wonder which style I shall try.

AN ATTACK OF SOCKETING

People who talk too much about their ailments are justly deemed to be bores. Yet there are one or two complaints the mention of which will, as a rule, produce a general and spirited conversation. If, for instance, one has anything the matter with one's knee or back and says so in company, one is at once overwhelmed by advice as diverse as it is sympathetic, since every one of the auditors knows the one man in the world who can cure knees and backs as if by magic. Similarly in the case of golfing ailments, almost every golfer has at some time or another had an attack of the fearful disease called "socketing," and will take his part in the talk if the latest victim starts the subject. Some, indeed, refrain not so much because they think the topic tiresome as because they think it too dreadful. Having been stricken and cured, they wish to forget all about the attack lest the mere thought of it should bring a recurrence. Such people had better skip the rest of this article, because I propose to describe a short, or at least I hope short, and severe attack of socketing which lately befell a golfer whose game I know better than I do anyone else's in the world.

This golfer, who has played the game now for a depressingly long time, has never been seriously troubled by socketing. He once had a mild visitation, in consequence of which he bought a crook-necked mashie and mashie-niblick supposed to make impossible the hitting off a non-existent socket. He grew so fond of them that he has played with them ever since—that is, for twelve or thirteen years—and, in cases of extreme mental anguish, has even gone so far as to putt with the mashie. Just once, for the space of a shot or two, he discovered that it was possible to socket with the socketless club, but he has been practically immune from the disease. Suddenly, like a thunderbolt out of a blue sky, it descended on him.

I believe that pride nearly always comes before a fall in such cases, and my golfer was playing, or thought he was playing, rather well with that crook-necked mashie. He was hitting the ball with plenty of "nip" and confidence: he was in a complacent state of mind and inclined to take liberties. One day he went out into the field next door to his house to play a few shots for air and exercise. He had on a good many clothes, and his braces felt rather tight, but what did that matter? He knew he could hit the ball, and for a few minutes he did hit it so accurately that he was lost in admiration of the perfect grouping of the balls in the smallest possible space at just the point he was aiming at. Then without the least warning a ball sped skimming the grass in the direction of cover-point. He laughed—a little uneasily and artificially— and addressed himself to another ball. That one went nearer point than cover-point, and of the next dozen balls nine or ten did exactly the same thing.

Anybody who has ever suffered will know what were his sensations. He felt as if Heaven's worst curse had suddenly fallen on him and he had gone mad. In other respects he appeared to himself to be normal; the scenery had not changed; the field and the dripping trees and the depressed cows in one corner looked just as they had ten minutes before. The thing in his hand was almost certainly a mashie (warranted not to socket); the thing on the grass was a ball which he was addressing in what he believed to be his usual way; he was looking at it very hard and swinging very slow; and yet—there went another one, farther to the right than ever. The hour of lunch was approaching. When he went in to eat it, his family would probably discover that he was raving mad and would send for the doctor; he would be removed to an asylum. Meanwhile (O heavens! look at that one!) he must and would hit one ball not on the socket before the gong summoned him to his doom. In the nick of time a notion came into his disordered brain, and one, two, three balls were hit straight; his deportment at lunch was not detected as being insane; perhaps he was not mad, after all.

He rushed out again afterwards, having first taken off some of those superfluous garments, and, except for one horror, there were no more socketings; but he played each shot with a most elaborate carefulness, even as a drunken man speaks when he is uncertain of his powers of articulation. Whether he is really cured it is too early to say, and in any case it is doubtful whether he will ever be the same man again. The shock of that sudden visitation is not easily forgotten, and the undeniably humorous circumstances of his socketing with a socketless club will not mend matters. I am apprehensive about the poor fellow's future.

It is conceivable that others who have suffered may ask how the attack was cured. Well, I am not quite sure. Socketing comes and goes, and I have always observed that golfing doctors are chary of prescribing for it. "A medal winner," remarked Sir Walter Simpson, "unable to hit with any part except the socket of his iron is no uncommon phenomenon"; but he laid down no precise treatment. As far as I could discover in my poor friend's case, both his previous complacency and his superfluous clothing had something to do with it. Both because he was self-satisfied and because he had too many clothes on for proper swinging, he tried to hit the ball with too much wrist and too little of anything else. Also, I fancied that his right elbow was not clinging to his side as it ought, but flying out from the body on the way down. At any rate, it was by trying to be very stiff and to keep that elbow under control that he checked the pestilence; but, for all I know, both the cause of the attack and the manner of its arrest were really quite other than those I have described.

I recollect that a good while ago this poor man won a certain tournament. In one of the rounds the enemy had come to such sad grief at the last hole that my friend could not fail to win if he kept topping the ball down the middle of the course. He remarked to an onlooker: "Thank Heaven, I've got a mashie without a socket," and by trundling the ball in inglorious safety with this weapon he duly won. If he had known then what he has learned now I doubt whether he would ever have reached the green at all. Meanwhile, I do hope that, by describing his torments in such detail, I shall not have put socketing into somebody else's head, especially into the head of somebody who has socketless clubs. That would, I admit, be an impish, not to say a malignant thing to do.

A MUSICAL CURE

"If music be the food of golf, play on." So spoke Orsino in the play, or if it was not exactly that it was something very like it.

Doubtless he was alluding to the necessity for rhythm, that indefinable and elusive something the presence of which we recognise in the swings of the great, while we are too painfully aware of its absence in our own. It comes and goes and, as we get older and stiffer, it is apt to go for ever, but if by chance we have a fair day we are conscious that it has come faintly fluttering back, and for a moment we can "almost hear the beating of its wings." There is a traditional prescription for its recapture, which consists in swinging the club to a waltz tune. I had tried it long since, as I must have tried almost everything once, but had forgotten all about it till I came across it again in the work of a highly distinguished American teacher, Mr. Seymour Dunn. So away I went to a secret valley, a very muddy one in the season of rain, where no human eye could see my contortions nor human ear hearken to my carollings, and "'gad, there I was," as Jos Sedley once observed, "singing away like—a robin."

There are presumably many waltz tunes, but I could only think of two. The first was that eminently languorous one, title to me unknown, from "The Merry Widow"; the second, if it may be named with respect, was the tune of the hymn called "Happy birds that sing and fly," which at least sufficiently resembles a waltz. Between these two I was forced to alternate. I am no musician any more than I am a dancer, and prefer, if I sing at all, to have my notes drowned by the running waters of my morning bath or still better by the rattle and roar of a railway train, supposing that I have a carriage to myself. I fancy my singing, though here I may be flattering myself, to be not unlike that of Bertie Wooster when he daily gave vent to "Sonny Boy." For golfing purposes, however, that is rather an advantage than otherwise. Singers of this type, that is to say having naturally bad taste, no voice, and an imperfect ear, are given to a slow and sentimental sweetness long drawn out, and this lends itself admirably to the drowsy swing which we ought to cultivate.

I remember in the early stages of the War being at Aldershot when Sir Walford Davies (he was only Dr. then) kindly came down to teach the new army how to sing and form regimental choirs. He told his pupils not to sing "in the sloppy, Bank Holiday style," and a general and sheepish grin showed that the shot had gone home. Then he made them sing the Old Hundredth, which they did so lugubriously as to evoke the protest, "Now you know you wouldn't sing 'How's your lady friend' like that." Next "The Old Folks at Home" was greeted with the friendly sarcasm, "Oh, come, sloppier than that!" Finally they were drilled into singing with a briskness and crispness that a little while before would have seemed incredible.

Sir Walford was clearly in the right, if it be not impertinent to say so; but I feel like Bob Acres when he refused to follow Sir Lucius's duelling precepts, and said firmly, "By my valour, I will stand edgeways." Music is one thing and golf is another, and for the purposes of this golfing cure I doubt if it be possible to sing too sloppily. Let the patient get all the intolerable pathos he can out of "One little hut among de bushes," "When will I hear de bees a-humming," and all the other words of that heart-breaking and beloved song. He can scarcely have too many tears in his voice, hardly be too maudlin, so long as nobody can hear him. If he tries to be too brisk he may soon be snatching and snapping at the ball as badly as ever.

A waltz tune is, no doubt, the best, but I am disposed, though diffidently, to think that almost any tune will do good, so long as we sing or whistle it with sufficient languor. It is not necessary to go on with "The Merry Widow" till it drives us mad. One important thing is not to take a deep breath at the top of the swing and come down on the ball with too violent a burst of melody. Another is not to stop as we reach the ball but to finish, of course in a chaste and classical attitude, with the music still flowing evenly from our lips. I ought to add that Mr. Dunn prescribes the waltz tune primarily for acquiring a rhythmic swing with no ball there. When there is a ball and we are inclined to press and jerk at it, he suggests a different musical remedy—namely, to "whistle a continuous, low, even note all the way through the swing." He may be right; he probably is, but this whistling of one note is by comparison a dreary and for some of us a difficult business. Do let us have our tune and get a little fun out of the treatment!

It may be observed that with singular modesty I have said nothing of the effect of this cure upon the particular patient in question. Well, hope does not spring as it did, and to hit the ball nowadays, if he ever does hit it, appears rather an ironical circumstance. Yet I will say this, that now and again he did seem to attain to some vestige of a pause at the top of the swing and actually did follow through. Moreover, and this is always a cheerful sign, the remedy was reasonably effective on the second day, whereas most remedies only last for one. The weather and the valley being now alike unspeakable he is wondering whether a musical treatment indoors would be good for putting. There might be a measure of compensation in putting at the drawing-room table-legs when the household insists on listening to Bach on the wireless. But these musical people are so fussy; they say "Hush," and besides I doubt if Bach is quite the man for the job.

ON BEING DORMY

It is doubtful whether golf, or indeed life, has any sensation to offer equal to that of becoming dormy. It may be that we experience only a blessed relaxation after strain and feel comparatively good-natured towards the enemy, or again we may want to turn on him in savage exultation and shout, as Andrew Kirkaldy once did when he holed his putt at the Corner of the Dyke, "The door's shut now." In either case it is a moment of almost delirious bliss.

I have been racking my brains to think of anything corresponding to it in other games. I can only discover one example. In the fourth innings at cricket when the batting side have made the match a tie with one or more wickets to fall they may be said to be dormy. No other game or sport can produce that defiant certainty, that absolute of immunity. A man may be leading by 100 yards in a mile race with only 10 yards to go, but he *may* fall down in a fit. If I were to play Mr. Newman or Mr. Davis at billiards and my score were blank, as it inevitably would be, and the champion's was 9,999 and I were left with a double balk, the chances of my ultimate success would be negligible, and yet the impish fates might have something up their sleeves. But if (of course in receipt of a stroke a hole) I am dormy one on Mr. Bobby Jones, I am impregnable; I need not even touch wood to avert the evil chance; there is the exquisite rub.

If these emotions appear excessive I can best make my defence in the words of Mr. Malthus, the honorary member of the Suicide Club. "Fear is the strong passion; it is with fear that you must trifle, if you wish to taste the intensest joys of living. Envy me—envy me, sir," he added with a chuckle. "I am a coward!" Every time the Ace of Spades was dealt to another player Mr. Malthus enjoyed the quintessence of being dormy; he found the relief so intoxicating that, as we know, he "trifled once too often with his terrors" and drew the card of death at last.

It is one of the most ruthless things about almost every match-play tournament that there is no dormy. We may be five up with five holes to play, but there always looms the hideous possibility of all the five dropping away one by one, so that we have to totter out again to the nineteenth under the gaze of gloating eyes. To this rule of cruelty there is one blessed exception. If a match is halved in the Jubilee Vase or the Calcutta Cup at St. Andrews there is no prolonging of the misery, and both sides pass through into the next round. So in these kindly competitions we do not greatly care what happens so long as we avoid defeat; if we have a four-foot putt for the match on the home green we bend all our faculties to the task of laying the ball dead; if we are as many holes up as there are holes left to play we light a pipe and assume, without affectation, an air of almost inconceivable jauntiness. There have even been cases in which charitable persons have lain under suspicion of not trying to win, and only the most hostile feel seriously annoyed if they let victory slip. At any rate they have lived to fight another day.

In these peculiar circumstances we attain to the ultimate poignancy of dorminess and can really, as the word implies, go to sleep if we have a mind to it. For that very reason we are likely to finish with a modest steadiness, for the plain fact is that as a rule we are not sleepy enough. For the first hole after we have become dormy a pleasant drowsiness sets in, and that will very likely enable us to get the half we want; but if we lose one hole we are apt to get restive, and if we lose two or three terror seizes us by the throat. We come to feel that nothing but a mistake by the other side will save us, and despite our prayers it is just at that moment that the beasts will not make a mistake. Sometimes, but not often, luck comes to our aid, and I am still fondly hugging to myself the memory of a certain rot-stopping long putt. I don't think the ball deserved to go in; it was struck only with the courage of despair: if it had not hit the exact back of the hole it must have jumped out again, but—ha! ha!—it stayed in, and once again the sky was blue and the larks were singing.

Other epicures in sensation may not agree, but I am disposed to think that the instant of sudden realisation that we are going to be dormy is sometimes better than that in which the impossible has really happened. A foursome of a few days ago comes gratefully to mind. After toiling and struggling and being down, we had by some incredible means become all square with two to go, and then my partner played a second shot of a quality so dazzling that my eyes are still blinded by the glory of it. I knew where the foe was—an agreeably horrid place—but I could not see our ball upon the green. "Where is it?" I cried in an agony, and a trusty friend walking with me replied, "It's so near the hole that even you can't help putting it dead." That was the supreme moment, and not the later one in which the ball, tremulously pushed towards the hole, did actually lie dead.

By some mischance this lovely word "dormy" has become partially corrupted in its passage across the Atlantic. I judge so at least, because I have now and again read in American golfing magazines that A was dormy three when it appears from internal evidence that in fact B was three up on him with three holes to play. How this inversion arose I cannot explain, but those who are guilty of it have wholly failed to grasp the beauty of the word. It is the only one in our language which signifies that for one transcendent moment we can snap our fingers under the nose of Fate.

ON USING OUR HEADS

We have long since been told on the authority of a famous caddie, Lang Willie, that "ye maun hae a heid to play gowf"; but it must be remembered that all things are comparative and that Lang Willie was contrasting golf with the particular employment of "learning thae lads at College Latin and Greek." We have all at times had cause to doubt whether his statement holds good in the abstract and whether we should not have done better without such heads as we possess.

Here, for instance, is the story of a recent experience, and I submit that it is not an egotistical one, since much the same thing has at some time happened to everybody. My partner and I in a foursome were two up going to the fourteenth hole. One of our adversaries had the kindness to slice his second far over a fence in the direction of an observatory; that was out of bounds, and they then played their fourth shot and were still some way short of the green. It was beyond my puny power to reach the green with a brassy, and there was a cross-bunker in the way, whereupon I safely carried the bunker with an iron and left my partner with a pitch or run-up to the green; we were nearly sure to take five and they were likely to take seven, and all was going as merrily as a marriage bell.

At this point one of the enemy called to me in a tone of friendly insult, "I see you're using your head." I accepted the compliment, with a modest feeling of having deserved it; I had no presentiment, no feeling of having been bewitched or "overlooked," but mark the sequel. My noble, long-suffering and magnificent partner, who had been hauling me round by the scruff of the neck, had a sudden lapse and hit the ball a trifling distance along the ground. The enemy responded with a perfect shot as near as might be stone dead; we had a putt for five, but the ball declined to go in; the hole was halved in six, and, incidentally, one of the very best of matches was in the end halved also.

A dull story, it may be said, and unduly spun out, but how typical of golf and how agonising! I cannot say that the tragedy kept me awake that night, but I did wonder what would have happened if I had done the wrong thing instead of the right thing, and whether perhaps I really did the wrong thing. Had I hit a good brassy shot, we should, humanly speaking, have had a five, and even if I had put the ball into the bunker we should probably have done no worse than six; but how essentially futile are such wonderings, and who can say what might have happened? If the Fates meant my partner to make that one mistake, he might have missed a shorter pitch just as he did a longer one, and, moreover, it is open to our enemies to say that they might have holed their pitch instead of merely laying it dead.

Nineteen times out of twenty no doubt things would have gone "according to plan"; we should have won that hole, and there is to my mind something especially satisfactory in winning a hole by careful tactics. Yet this using of the head has its psychological disadvantages; it tells the enemy that we are afraid of him and afraid of ourselves. In this particular case the enemy needed no telling, for he had lately lopped two holes off our lead of four and was pressing us hard, but in any case enemies are cheered by seeing us cautious and are apt to put in a thrust accordingly. To have taken a brassy instead of an iron would have been an overt act of defiance, of confidence, if not felt at least simulated. When in the converse instance, our adversary, regardless of our misfortunes, goes boldly for the flag, we hope that he is being a fool, but we are at the same time conscious that he is not so frightened of us as we should like him to be.

To take another illustration, there are in golf few gestures more splendid and challenging than that of the man who is one or two up and sets out to pitch a stymie for the hole. He can have a half for the asking and keep his lead, but he refuses to fear his fate too much. Frightful things may obviously befall him; he may pitch too far and run out of holing; he may knock the other ball in and stay outside himself. Yet even if the worst happens he has shown the enemy what he thinks of him, and that is something; it may even be everything.

I was re-reading the other day Mr. Hilton's reminiscences, and in it there is a small story on this point, from the Amateur Championship at Sandwich in 1900. Mr. Maxwell had just won the St. George's Vase; he was playing his most alarming game, and Mr. Hilton had to meet him on the second day of the championship. Mr. Hilton was one up going to the Maiden; he would have had a short putt for the hole, but was laid a dead stymie with his opponent's ball only an inch or so from the hole. "Had I knocked him in," he says, "as I certainly should have done had I hit his ball, I should have lost a hole which I had every right to win. In addition to the actual loss of the hole there was also the moral effect to take into account as, although the match was still in its comparative infancy, it was certainly at a critical stage." He went for the shot, holed it and so was two up; he at once holed a good putt at the next hole, and that was three up; he won the match comfortably on the fifteenth green, and in the end he won the championship. The defying of that stymie may well have changed golfing history.

The moral effect that we produce on our opponents is often important, but scarcely so important as that which we produce on ourselves. The golfer ought to be the best judge of his own temperament; he may know by experience that a risk taken with disastrous results is likely to upset him, whereas a conservative policy resolutely pursued gives him a comfortable and steadying sensation of not having made a fool of himself. In that case he is wise to use what he is pleased to call his head. If, on the other hand, he is one of the lucky ones, who can dismiss the dreadful past, he is right to take the more dashing and glorious course. The thing to avoid at all costs is the recurring thought: "It was and hadn't oughter be." If we know ourselves to be but poor hands at doing so, then we must do our cautious and contemptible best to avoid giving it cause to haunt us. Perhaps that is what Lang Willie meant. At any rate I have no regrets; I should take my iron again.

NINE HOLES

It is, I suppose, largely a sentimental love for the past that makes me regret that there are now so very few nine-hole courses. In the golfing directories the number of holes is still given among the particulars of each club, but it is almost a matter of form. One may read through the list for page after page before lighting, with a Rip Van Winkle sensation, on the entry "9 holes."

How many such courses do I know? There is Worlington, of course, as I think the best of all inland golf, which, please goodness, never, never, never shall have eighteen holes. There is a very charming subsidiary course of nine holes at Frilford Heath. There is Hampstead, now one of the most venerable of London courses, where I used to play with an old friend some thirty something years ago. There is the engaging cat's cradle of Bembridge, but I have not seen it for such a very long time that it has almost faded. There is—how dare I name it last!—historic Musselburgh. But, then, Musselburgh is almost an illustrious ghost nowadays and I have never played over it; I have but pulled up for a moment or two on the road between Edinburgh and North Berwick and looked at it with eyes at once reverent and wondering. There are to be sure one or two charming private courses, but the one I loved best, Kinshaldie, where one played Sabbath-breaking rounds from St. Andrews, now lies solitary behind its curtain of woods, having gone back to nature and the rabbits, unkempt, unplayed on, but not unwept.

Golf has become too popular for nine-hole courses to exist. Even at Worlington, which is peaceful and lonely enough, the players on a match-day resemble a whiting eating its own tail. The first foursome hole out on the home green, as the last is driving from the first tee, and the poor wretches who are not playing in the match swear great oaths at the selfishness of those who are, and wonder how in the world they are ever going to squeeze their way into the procession. The inevitable march of things cannot be stopped by regrets, and yet it is a pity, for there is many a good golf course that has been spoilt by having been turned from nine holes into eighteen. That course may be called fortunate that, having nine good holes, has not another yard of ground to spare and so cannot be changed even by the most ingenious and utterly ruinous criss-crossing.

Nine holes can grow tiresome no doubt, but if we do not play them too often there is a great deal to be said for them. For one thing they are most companionable: we constantly see our friends and "hail one another in passing." As we are playing the sixth along one side of the avenue of firs, they are going to the eighth along the other side, and we may even meet on the common ground of trouble among the tree trunks. It is true that nine holes have the defect of their qualities, and there is not often to be found on them the romantic scenery and solitude such as we enjoy, for instance, among the hills and valleys of Sandwich; but on the whole I think I like the friendliness best, unless, indeed, I am so many holes down that I wish to look no man in the face or answer any of his questions as to my welfare. There is friendliness, too, in the fact that the club-house comes in the middle of the match: that friendliest of all men, dear Mr. Pickwick, would have liked to play on a nine-hole course, to have sheltered for a moment from the bitter wind and drunk cherry brandy between the rounds. There is a truly Pickwickian quality of snugness and cosiness about nine holes which is lacking in the greater spaces of eighteen.

Again it is pleasant, even if it be also alarming, to face twice in each match and four times in the day the great holes of a course. It is good fun to try as soon as may be to conquer them again if we have failed the first time. If we have succeeded the first time it is good for the soul to conquer that still small voice within us which whispers fatalistically "I can never do it again." The old round at Felixstowe ended with two tremendous holes, Bunker's Hill and The Point, and to tackle them four times, if each time was vitally important, was "wery fierce"; yet there was a splendour about it too. I wonder how it would be if we had to do the same with the Road Hole at St. Andrews. Would our nerves utterly give out or would familiarity breed not contempt—that could never be—but a slightly less appalling respect?

I have a particularly tender-hearted feeling for nine-hole courses because the memories of my boyhood's golf are largely bound up with three of them. The three were Felixstowe, Cromer and Eastbourne; I saw them all turn into eighteen holes, and I think that in each case the change was certainly not for the better and almost certainly for the worse. I also played at Aberdovey when there were but nine holes, before Cader existed, and we had a long tramp on the high road to the railway crossing and began by playing to the present fifth green. That, however, was almost in the days of flower-pots in the holes, before the course officially existed at all, and in this case there was ample room for eighteen holes and the change was all to the good.

It is only natural to feel a conservative affection for the courses of one's youth, if only because one was then growing, as Dr. Coué might have said, every day and in every way better and better and longer and longer, not shorter and shorter and worse and worse. Yet, at any rate, as regards one of the three I have mentioned, there is, I think, but one opinion amongst those who knew Felixstowe that it was very good golf indeed. Those last two holes constituted its chief glory, but there were others that were both good and attractive; the ground had in it the true golfing folds and undulations and the turf was beautiful, of a true seaside fineness not often to be seen nowadays. Then the sea was so close and so delightfully visible, not hidden away behind sand-hills, and the Martello tower so romantic. It stood on one side of the first green; Willie Fernie's shop was on the other, and the fourth green was close by, so that the whole made up an essentially cheerful meeting and watching place. However, I am conscious of having too often sentimentalised about Felixstowe and will leave it and turn to Cromer.

After three or four years of a family holiday in Suffolk we went in 1889 to Cromer, and there, just after my thirteenth birthday, I holed the nine holes in 49 shots, a feat which bumped my head against the stars. At least I said I did, and

I have really no reason to doubt my youthful word; yet I have sometimes twinges of conscience; it was a very good score for me and one or two of the putts may not have been holed out. At any rate, I was not playing by myself, as was often my custom, but with another rather older boy, Willie Aveston, who afterwards became a very good professional golfer; so let us hope those putts were holed.

There were some very odd holes at Cromer but they were amusing, and the turf of the old nine was good. It was not the genuine seaside article, since the course was on the top of a cliff, but neither was it the too genuine inland article on which were made the new holes. It was, as I remember it, such turf as is found on commons, and there were gorse bushes and bracken which are also found on commons. In short, the course was a golf course and not a field. It began at the bottom of a deep dell and the first drive was up a grassy gorge with rough and bracken on either side. Then came a blind second shot to a green on the top, surrounded by turf walls, something after the manner of the Cops at Hoylake. After that we played to a green under the shadow of the light-house (where Willie Aveston lived, for his father was the light-house keeper), and then we went plunging down into a valley with gorse and bracken on either hand. There was a good deal of plunging down and then toiling up again, and the last green was at the bottom of the dell where we had started. We hit down to it from the heights above, and I remember that there was a story of a famous professional who had been given a brassy to play the shot and had carried green, club-house and all. He was said to have told the caddie that he "did na ken gowf," and this sounded in my young southern ears a fearful curse.

In those days there was a tiny little ladies' course along the top of the cliff, but the cliff was always crumbling and tumbling and, when I came back to Cromer as an undergraduate five or six years later, all the ladies' course had vanished into the German Ocean: so had most of the eighth green, and now nearly all the old first green has followed it down the precipice. Its grass walls could not save it. It was fun to come back again as a grown-up player of grown-up shots and to marvel pityingly at the shortness of one's old ones, but I never could love the new ground as I had loved the old, and now the club-house has grown and moved and there is no playing in or out of that deep dell, and when the wind is blowing, the ghosts of the old holes walk abroad in the storm.

None of the Eastbourne nine holes have fallen over a cliff: some at least of them seemed to be unchanged when I took a walk on the course some years ago, and I think I could almost find my way blindfold to the sites of the old lost greens. I do not know that some of those holes were very exciting or very interesting, or in fact very anything that holes ought to be. At the first two or three I cannot remember any particular hazards, except starveling patches of gorse protected by hurdles, and I can still feel myself getting exceedingly angry as I hear the sound of a hurdle being bombarded by my ball. There was to be sure the danger of slicing and making a Gadarene descent on the right-hand side, a danger made graver by the fierce winds that blew; but there was nothing very exciting till we drove over the chalk-pit at the fourth and so home, over Paradise Wood if we were brave and round it if we were cautious, to the horseshoe green with the Greek temple looking down on it. I used to like the fifth in my unsophisticated way, though I daresay I should now pour contempt on it as a "gun-platform green"; and I am sure the eighth was a good hole, a bending hole along the edge of Compton Place, where a drifting tee shot, risking the trees and the ha-ha beneath them, could mean an exquisite thrill—or out-of-bounds.

The greens were, as I remember them, good in their way, but it was an essentially deceptive way, and the local player was greatly to be feared on them. It was almost impossible to borrow too much, dreadfully easy to borrow too little, and how the ball did trickle on and on when the chalky ground was hard and burnt in a hot summer! This necessity for borrowing was not confined to the putting; approaching was anything but a plain-sailing, straightforward art, and it was well summed up in the local golfing proverb that "the ball always comes back from Beachy Head." One or two of the greens, moreover, had side walls, and these could be deftly used to the confounding of the stranger.

Apart from my father, my mind is now rather a blank as to the people with whom I used to play. I think some of them must have been Colonels, because I remember that once the professional, Peter Paxton, in a moment of irritation against the Committee, exclaimed, "The place fair stinks with half-pay officers." One of my adversaries I do recall vividly and gratefully. He was not a Colonel, but a Captain in the Navy with a red beard. He beat me and I did not, and still do not, think he ought to have done so. I am afraid I made this view all too clear, whereupon he very kindly said, "Remember, this round is not an examination on which your whole future life depends." That was as good a piece of advice as I have ever been given in my life, and I have often and often wished that I could have profited by it.

We went to Eastbourne for several consecutive summers so that I was getting quite old towards the end of them, and one glorious day I played a gentleman who was a member of the Cambridge team. He wore the beautiful red coat with a light blue collar which I was later to wear myself; I beat him and that was a terrific moment; I walked home, up the hill and across the sixth fairway and over the stile, in a state of unutterable complacency. The great Horace was an Eastbourne golfer in those days, but I think he was seldom there in the summer, and I can only remember seeing him once or twice on the course. Once, as he passed me, he said in a kind and Olympian manner that I had made a good shot; then, to make my feelings if possible more poignant, he made rather a bad one himself. I could walk to the place now, blindfolded.

After I had gone up to Cambridge the family holiday was never spent at Eastbourne again; indeed, I think it came to be spent abroad and I, resolutely refusing to go where there was no golf, was left to play at home. I have only once played at Eastbourne in all the years since—in a match against Sussex—but I still hold it in affectionate remembrance. I still have a conviction, which would be painfully and easily disproved, that were I now suddenly put down on one of those old greens I should know by instinct the number of yards that I must aim towards Beachy Head. And I know as well as I know anything that

I should be frightened of topping my tee shot into that pit in the depths of which I so often delved with youthful imprecations amid the chalk.

ARCHITECTOORALOORAL

Joe Gargery, it may be remembered, was disappointed when on his visit to London he went to see the blacking warehouse; he thought that in the pictures of it which he had previously seen it had been "drawd too architectooralooral."

There are some who would, I fancy, if they knew it, apply this word of Joe's to the designers of golf courses. They think that these gentlemen have become a little too ingenious and too subtle, and are inclined to yearn for the simpler architecture of old times. On very rare occasions, as regards some particular piece of cleverness that has a little missed its mark, I agree with this view, but on the whole I most decidedly disagree with it. I have a great admiration for our golfing architects, and when we are inclined to criticise them or their works it would be well if we paused to consider what sort of a hand at it we should make ourselves. There was a time when the nearest professional player was deemed fully qualified to lay out a new course, and any body of retired colonels, constituting a green committee, thought that they could at the very least make a new hole. This state of pristine innocence is not often to be found to-day, but I doubt whether the average golfer even now fully realises that the professional architect is not merely likely, but certain, to do the job infinitely better than the casual amateur just because it is his job, that he is paid to think about it, and has thought about it a great deal.

Those who laid out courses when the first great golf "boom" came did not presumably think much, neither had they very suitable equipment for thinking purposes. They had the material for thought in certain famous holes on famous courses, but they entirely failed, if they ever tried, to analyse the qualities of those holes and to discover wherein their merits lay. They took, as a rule, the way of least resistance;

if they saw a hill they drove over it, and a hollow was clearly designed by Providence for a green, although oddly enough that same Providence had put most of the greens at St. Andrews upon plateaux. It seems to me that the great and primary virtue of the modern architect lies in the fact that he did analyse: that he went back to the classic models, and especially to St. Andrews, and insisted on discovering why golfers had for years particularly enjoyed playing particular holes. It is obvious by way of example that nobody ever gets tired of playing the sixteenth hole—the Corner of the Dyke. In what does its peculiar charm lie? Certainly not in the fact that the Principal's Nose punishes a bad shot because as a rule it punishes rather a good one, in the sense of a shot that is more or less cleanly hit. The charm is in the fact that the hole keeps us, unconsciously perhaps, thinking, that we have always got to make up what we are pleased to call our minds; that we have to decide between, on the one hand, a highly dangerous but highly profitable course that may lose us several strokes but may gain us one invaluable stroke, and, on the other, a comparatively safe, easy course that ought not to lose us much but may just lose us something intensely important. Their discoveries came, I think, very briefly to this, that golf at its best is a perpetual adventure, that it consists in investing not in gilt-edged securities but in comparatively speculative stock; that it ought to be a risky business.

Here was something of a new belief founded upon old holes. How those old holes attained the form in which we know them no one can tell. Assuredly it was not owing to the genius of some one heaven-sent designer whose name has unjustly been lost. It was rather through good fortune and a gradual process of evolution. The holes changed their forms many times according as whins grew or were hacked away, according as the wind silted up sand here or blew it away there, according as the instruments of the game changed so that men could hit farther and essay short cuts and new roads. Yet they possessed some indestructible virtue, so that, however they changed superficially, golfers united in praising them and loved to play them, gaining from the playing of them some pleasing emotion that other holes could not afford. To define that emotion and the cause of it was really to make a discovery, and to proclaim the discovery was to proclaim a new faith.

It was Mr. John Low who first put this faith into memorable words, and they are so excellent that I will set them down again here. He is defending the little pot-bunker that is very nearly on the bee-line to the hole and, he says, "The greedy golfer will go too near and be sucked in to his destruction. The straight player will go just as near as he deems safe, just as close as he dare. Just as close as he dare: that's golf, and that's a hazard of immortal importance! For golf at its best should be a contest of risks. The fine player should on his way round the links be just slipping past the bunkers, gaining every yard he can, conquering by the confidence of his own 'far and sure' play. The less skilful player should wreck himself either by attempting risks which are beyond his skill, or by being compelled to lose ground through giving the bunkers a wide berth."

Those words were written in 1903, and it was just about that time, I think, and, generally speaking, in accordance with the beliefs so proclaimed that the two leaders of the new school of architecture, Mr. H. S. Colt and Mr. Herbert Fowler, were doing their work. Yet if one hole has to be taken as typifying these beliefs, it is not one designed by either of them, but by a distinguished amateur. The hole is the fourth at Woking, which is familiar to all who look out of the railway carriage window as they go from Waterloo towards Southampton, and its designer was Mr. Stuart Paton, who is well-known to all who ever played on the Woking course, and has even been designated by an irreverent writer its Mussolini. This was, when I first knew it, a comparatively commonplace hole. The tee shot had to be played between the railway on the right and the heather on the left, and there was a sufficiently wide stretch of fairway between them. The green was guarded by a cross bunker which covered its entire width. A tolerably straight drive and a tolerably adroit pitch were wanted, and nothing more.

Mr. Paton, presumably reminded by the railway line of the sixteenth hole at St. Andrews, saw his opportunity and proceeded to plant a Principal's Nose in the shape of a double bunker in the middle of fairway. He reduced the cross bunker,

I rather think by stages, until nothing was left of it but one small pot in the middle of the edge of the green. Thus the man who courageously lays down his balls between the first bunker and the railway line gets a clear run up to the hole on the most favourable possible terms. The more cautious one who drives to the left can still get his four, but, owing to the contour of the green, he has a much more difficult approach to play. He will find himself hampered by that second central bunker. If he pitches over it, he will have hard work to stop his ball from running away into trouble; if he dare not pitch but plays a running shot, he will often leave himself a long, nasty sloping putt.

From being a cut-and-dried affair, the hole became an uncommonly interesting and provocative one, and one which a man is always glad to leave safely behind him in a medal round. Moreover, since it was certainly one of the first, if not the first, of its kind in southern architecture, it roused plenty of hostility and plenty of argument. Its enemies said that the drive that was caught by the bunker in the middle of the course was invariably a very good drive, and that therefore the bunker was unfair. Its friends replied that the bunker was there, that the player knew it was there, and that it was his business to avoid it. The drive might have been a very good one if there had been no bunker there; as things were it was not a good enough one. The argument goes on to this day; people still abuse the hole, and if any further evidence be required of its merits it is to be found in that persistence of calumny. All the great holes and great bunkers of the world have their puny enemies.

I have mentioned this hole not only because it came something before its time and so shared the fate of zealots and reformers in being abused. It had in another way an effect impossible exactly to measure on modern golf. It plays something of the part in the story of a distinguished architect which the cakes are supposed to have played in the story of King Alfred. One day Mr. Simpson, who was then a good golfer but had never designed a hole in his life, went over to Woking for a game of golf. The day turned pitilessly wet and golf was out of the question. Whether the conversation among those storm-bound in the club-house actually turned on the fourth hole or whether Mr. Simpson had heard such talk before I am not certain. At any rate, he determined to go and look critically at that hole. So out he went in solitude and a mackintosh, and, with the rain pouring off him, devoted his "immense and brooding spirit" to considering the purpose of that little bunker in the middle of the course. When at last he came in again, wet but presumably happy, he had found a new interest in life. He became, as all the world now knows, a golfing architect, one of the straitest sect, of an almost diabolically ingenious mind, who loves to see what the thoughtless golfer calls a good shot go bang into a bunker which is ready to receive it. As we ply our niblicks in one of his creations let us remember with gratitude what we owe indirectly to Mr. Paton and the fourth hole at Woking!

No man can be a good architect unless he has a wide experience of many courses, a most observant eye for the weaknesses of his brother golfers, and red-hot zeal for his art, so that he is more interested in seeing other people play holes than in playing them himself. And beyond this he must possess that indefinable, instinctive something that may be called an eye for country. There are some courses which may be said to lay themselves out in so far as this, that the rough outline at once suggests itself to any experienced golfer. Even so that is not very far on the road to success, and the experienced golfer would generally fail to get the best, or anything like the best, out of his ground. As a rule, however, the circumstances are not nearly so favourable; the architect finds himself plumped down in the middle of a wood and can go north, south, east or west as it pleases him. The ordinary person would feel himself lost, throwing up his hands in despair, and it is then, I suppose, that the natural instinct of the born architect comes to the rescue.

I have at different times spent very interesting days with eminent architects upon the sites of their labours when those labours had scarcely begun—with Mr. Colt at Stoke Poges and St. George's Hill, with the late Mr. Abercromby at Coombe Hill and Addington. I have called those days interesting; I should have said awe-inspiring, so bewildered was my own state of mind, so lucid and determined was that of my companion. I would be shown a thicket so dense that we had to struggle through it with a motion of men swimming, and be told that this was the line to the first hole. The line might, for all I knew, have just as well been in a precisely opposite direction. Yet I fancy that if two architects had been set to work, their instinct would have guided them to start through that particular thicket and no other; indeed I am told, though I cannot give chapter and verse for it, that the experiment has been tried, and the two consultants arrived independently, not merely at the same beginning, but at much the same entire round.

The piece of architectural vision which most of all impressed me is to-day represented by that admirable short hole, the seventh, at Stoke Poges. When I first went there with its creator, Mr. Colt, all that met my vacant gaze was a steep uniform slope thickly covered with wood running down to a small stream. To have seen concealed in that apparently most unpromising material a long, narrow, plateau green with a bunkered slope on the one side, and a deep drop into the perdition of the stream on the other still strikes me as an effort of genius.

In such cases there is nothing for it but to reflect humbly that, after all, it is the architect's job, and that it is only natural that he should do it better than a mere casual student. Yet these confounded architects can sometimes put us to shame when we really do think that we are as good as they are. When Rye had to be altered, I was one of a Sub-Committee to consider possible changes. We thought hard and long: we devised a scheme and then we got Mr. Simpson to come and polish it up for us. We were particularly well pleased with our new first hole, and a very good hole I venture to say it is, but the humiliating part of the business was this, that Mr. Simpson had only to move half-a-dozen yards or so from the place we had designed for the green to find one obviously much better. We had pored over the site and he had not. Why had we not discovered that place that was plain for all to see, when it was pointed out? I do not know, and whatever I might admit on my own account I hesitate to say that all my companions were stupid. The fact remains that we had not. So I must needs say, "Hooroar for the architects."

I imagine that this altering and remodelling of courses is in fact a more delicate and difficult task than that of laying out a new one. The architect has neither so free a hand nor such agreeable privacy; everybody can see what he is at and can criticise accordingly. Moreover, he is sure to find himself opposed to vested interests in the shape of holes that have long and often undeservedly been regarded with love and veneration. This is particularly the case with blind one-shot holes which belong perhaps to the gutty era, when they were, at any rate, much more formidable than at present. I can still remember my feelings when a good many years ago I accompanied Mr. Colt on his advisory visit to Aberdovey. The third hole—it was then the fourth—is Cader, and the fact that it is the only hole habitually called by a name and not a number is eloquent. It calls for some sort of iron shot over a sandhill crowned with sleepers on to a hidden green with not unkindly sides. What would my companion say? He maintained a tactful silence that meant more than any words until he reached the far end of the green, when he said, "Take that back wall away." Then we passed on towards the next tee and, incidentally, that back wall is still there.

I have myself, I confess, a certain affection for Cader. I do not want it altered, and it is at least a far better hole than is the Maiden of Sandwich, possessing much more alarming trouble and a much smaller green. As compared with the Sandy Parlour at Deal, it is a perfect pearl among short holes. Will those more famous holes ever be altered? I gravely doubt it. Some little while ago there was a proposal to alter the Maiden by playing across the present green to a plateau perched high on the hilltop. There was, I believe, some prospect of the proposal being approved until an old friend of mine made a speech full of the most moving "sob stuff" about the dear old Maiden. The proposal was thereupon instantly and indignantly rejected. I do not say that either my friend or my fellow-members of the club were necessarily wrong, since I have in my own composition a good deal both of sentimentality and conservatism. I am only giving an illustration of the fact that reforming architects have to go warily.

They do go very warily, being as a rule monuments of tact. They can see deep into the frailties and vanities of the human heart, and can bamboozle green committees into doing their will. In short, they are great men, and they will have need to show themselves greater than ever in the years to come. It is their task to make golf courses no harder for the ordinary mortal, and yet a good deal more exacting and less monotonous for the man who can regularly drive untold yards and as regularly follow his drive with a high pitching shot with some lofted variety of graded iron. They have tackled it with courage and ingenuity, but it would be flattery to say that they have wholly succeeded, since the modern ball and the modern golfer's power of hitting it are in combination sometimes too much for them. A good illustration was to be found during the Open Championship of 1935 in the first hole at Muirfield. Here there has been made a highly ingenious little bunker some little distance in front of the green rather on the right-hand side of the fairway. Its object is to make the player place his tee shot to the left. In doing this he has to run an appreciable risk of going into a bunker, but, if he succeeds, he gets a clear run in to the hole with his second shot. If, on the other hand, he drives to the right, he must either carry that little bunker with his second or slice the ball skilfully round it. Everything goes according to plan for ordinary mortals, especially if the turf be not too keen and fast. The hole is then a good "two-shot hole," demanding accuracy as well as length. In the Open Championship, on the other hand, that little bunker entirely wasted its sweetness and might as well not have existed. With a light wind behind them player after player drove three hundred yards or more, and I saw, with my own eyes, Mr. Lawson Little hit a drive computed to be three hundred and sixty yards. The second shot became a pitch with a mashie-niblick, and whether or not it had to carry the little bunker was of no importance whatever. The ball and the hitter between them had rendered nugatory a very clever piece of architecture, and it is my present impression that, unless something be done to the ball, this combination will generally prove one too many for the architect.

The architects never say die; they return to the charge again and again with unimpaired bravery, they approach nearer and nearer to the kind of difficulty that is called "unfair." At the time when I am writing, the new course at Sunningdale, as altered by Mr. Simpson and Mr. Paton, is only just in play, and I can only write about it as I saw it in the rough. They seem to me to have gone further than anyone has gone yet in insisting on the "laying down" of the tee shot in a particular place; they have certainly made some admirable and interesting holes, but it remains to be seen how far they have succeeded, and whether or not the ball will beat them after all.

As far as I can see, the architect's strongest and most faithful ally in this perpetual battle is the plateau green. It cannot prevent the length of a hole being spoiled and its character impaired, but it can prevent its becoming child's play. The best example I can think of is the long hole in, the fourteenth, at St. Andrews, universally recognised as one of the few great long holes. If we are to see it at its best, the player must skirt the Beardies with his tee shot down the Elysian Fields; play his second to the left of Hell bunker and as near as he dare to it, and so attain the ideal position for his third, a run-up shot. If the ground is hard and there is a following wind, the long driver upsets all these well-laid plans; he drives miles and miles down the Elysian Fields without bothering his head about Beardies, and goes straight for the green with his second, carrying far over Hell, probably with an iron. The old game of going from point to point has gone; "geography has been destroyed," as I have heard Mr. Robert Harris exclaim in a passionate tirade; but there does remain that narrow plateau green with a steep bank in front of it, a run-away at the back, and hills, that will make a fool of almost any shot and any player, on its right-hand side. Even if the long driver plays his second with a mashie, he will have hard work to stay on the green; he is at least as likely to take five as four. That is small compensation perhaps for the destruction of the true beauty of the hole, but it is at least some amends. The hole's character may be changed, but the hole is not conquered; it still defies the player.

I am conscious that I seem to be writing as if I had a hatred of long drivers and was suffering from a disease to be briefly described as "sour grapes." This is not really so. I am the last person to want golf to become a less athletic game. Long driving is not merely a matter of youth and strength; it is essentially a matter of skill and deserves every fair advantage it can gain. At present it is doing more than that; it is spoiling the beauty and interest of the game. In consequence there seems to me a real danger lest architects should conceive an unjustifiable enmity against the long hitters and should be driven to be too subtle and too malignant in their efforts to curb the slasher. A hole can be too clever and so can defeat its own end. I do not know many examples, but I think I could name one or two. We decidedly want golf courses to be tests of accuracy and forethought, and even perhaps a little low cunning as well as of mere straightforward hitting, but we do not want the game, as described in "The Golfers' Manual," of "oldsters spooning a ball gently on to a table of smooth turf when a longer shot would land them in grief."

The architects have done nobly; they have fought the good fight, but it ought not to be a fight. The fact that it threatens to become so is the fault of the ball. Whether or not the ball can ever be brought back to its proper limits is another story, but unless it can, the architects will be for ever fighting an uphill battle.

A MID-WINTER NIGHT'S DREAM

Epithets are important, though it is doubtless still more important to do without them. We have to be particular at this season about the epithets for Christmas and the New Year—the one merry and the other happy. It would never do to transpose them, since we would scarcely wish our worst enemies a whole year of merriment. If we played golf on Christmas Day it is to be hoped that we put into it a reasonable amount of the carnival spirit; but imagine twelve whole months of back-slapping, leg-pulling, cheerio-drinking, four-ball matches. The mere thought sheds a melancholy upon the soul, and so we must be careful to wish each other a happy golfing New Year.

It is, of course, a vain wish. The only golfer that could truly be called happy would be some poor gentleman who went round the links with a keeper under the delusion that he was Bobby Jones. Short of that there can only be different degrees of unhappiness. At this moment I almost believe myself to be happy, because I hope to be playing golf on New Year's Day. Yes, if all goes well, I shall be snuffing the sea breeze and teeing my ball at just about the hour when suburban trains, having possibly been delayed by fog, are disgorging their freight of toilers at some bleak terminus. Yet I do not say this in any gloating or offensive spirit. Those black-coated golfers, though they may not realise it, will be happy for a longer period of the New Year than I shall. Not till the Saturday morning will their hopes be blasted, whereas the gorgeous fabric of my dream will have been unravelled by lunch-time on Tuesday.

The best I can wish any fellow golfer is that at this the last week-end of the old year he may discover a something, no matter what, which is to make him a new man for evermore. Let him discover it not while waggling a delusive poker in his room or even at practice with a club and ball in his garden. Let it be while he is playing a real game against a flesh-and-blood opponent; and I would pass him the further hint that he had better light on it as late as possible, so that it may last out the round. Then he can think about it continuously as he smokes his cigar after dinner on Sunday night, and spasmodically, so far as his workaday avocations permit, during Monday, Tuesday, Wednesday, Thursday, and Friday. After that the deluge; he will at least have enjoyed the maximum of un-clouded happiness during the New Year.

Is there any other game which produces in the human mind such enviable insanity? Does, for instance, the Rugby football player, as he goes to bed on the 31st of December, hug to himself the belief that he will never again miss a place-kick at goal because of some nonsense or other that has just been revealed to him? A place-kick right in front of goal is rather like a short putt, and many a golfer on New Year's Eve believes that he will never miss a short putt again. I do not know, but I very much doubt, if the football player shares this touching conviction. There is, to be sure, a difference between the two cases. The golfer is entirely dependent on himself, and so it is enough if he have complete faith in himself. In the case of the football player and his kick there is the other fellow who lies on his stomach in the mud and may place the ball with tremulous and bungling fingers. There are also those nasty rough creatures who wait beneath the cross-bar ready to rush out; they, too, may interfere with the perfect kick. So the analogy is defective and there remains only the billiards player who may imagine that never again will he miss a half-ball loser from balk. At least, I suppose he may, but, having never yet learnt where to tee my ball for that apparently simple shot, I find such a state of mind hard to conceive.

The golfer may be more at the mercy of this mid-winter night's dream because he can have a new club or even, in these prodigal times, a whole set of new clubs. The football player has no weapons but those Nature has given him, and I cannot think—perhaps this is mere ignorance or preju-dice—that a new cue or bat or racket can flood the mind with the same glow of madness as does a new club. Only the other day, I met a distinguished golfer of my acquaintance who takes the game, as a rule, in the spirit of a philosopher at once lighthearted and cynical. Yet it was with a radiant face and almost a blush that he told me that a set of wooden clubs with extremely springy shafts had given him a fresh lease of life and that he had gone round his home course in sixty-nine. Now it happens that this particular golfer has also enjoyed a second blooming as a cricketer. He does not, however, attribute that pleasing fact to a new bat, but to sitting at the feet of a wise man. A bat can be a very good bat, but even on New Year's Eve, when fairies are abroad, it cannot pretend to be a magic wand.

Perhaps, then, I ought to add to my New Year's good wishes to the reader that somebody may give him a new club. There was once a small girl who on being promised a puppy as a present asked whether she might get under the table to think about it. My imaginary reader may not wish to go to that length, but, if the club be a putter, he can at least practise with it at the legs of the table. If he does not fall into the vulgar error of not hitting hard enough he will be sure to hit them, and his five days of beautiful, foolish, pathetic hopes will thereby be made if possible more beautiful than ever.

MORNING OR AFTERNOON

A little while ago I took part, during a delightful week-end, in two team matches. On the first day the programme laid down for us consisted of foursomes in the morning and singles in the afternoon. We duly played our foursomes and had an admirable lunch. Then, with the temperature something over eighty in the shade (only there was no shade), the prospect of singles appeared a grim one. I and another rather elderly member of the side made ourselves at once so piteous and so unpleasant that foursomes were played again. News of our reprehensible and insidious conduct reached the neighbouring course where we were to play our second match, and the authorities there were resolute. When we arrived on a still hotter day we found the order of battle uncompromisingly set out on the notice board with singles in the morning. We bowed to the inevitable; each of the two principal villains won his single—a fact which brought some balm—and when we came in to lunch—scrumptious!—we felt that we had broken the back of the day's work and that a comparatively placid afternoon lay before us.

I have set out at length these possibly discreditable facts (it really was *very* hot) because there seems to me much to be said for reverting to the old fashion of singles first and foursomes afterwards. To-day this old order is nearly always reversed and the foursomes come first. The arguments for doing this are familiar and not unsound. The chief of them is the maintaining of the match's interest. It sometimes happens that one side gains such a lead in the singles, as to be dormy, or nearly so, before the foursomes begin, and that makes one side feel rather lazy and the other rather hopeless. Again it may be urged that the visiting players who do not know the course ought to have the chance of learning it as little expensively as possible, and that they can lose fewer points through their ignorance if the foursomes come first. On the other hand, I think nobody can pretend that to play the foursomes first is anything but a reversal of the natural sequence of events. A single when we are fresh and vigorous in the morning, a foursome when we feel a little less energetic and a little more mellow after lunch—this is surely the order in which the average golfer contemplates his day's golf; nor are his sentiments materially altered by the fact that his game is called a match, and the honour of his club is resting, not as a rule too heavily, upon his shoulders.

In the case of a match lasting two days, such as the Walker Cup or the University match, this last consideration does not apply and things may well be left as they are. It is a sad thought that if the singles had come first in the Walker Cup match of 1934—or in some other years, for that matter—the American side would not have been dormy, they would have been five up with four to play, and the foursomes would have been merely a bye. The match would have been even flatter and more dismal than it in fact was. I am thinking rather of the everyday team match, pleasant, friendly, and of no epoch-making importance. Personally, I believe that such matches should be played entirely by foursomes, both because foursomes import as far as possible the team element into that which is not a team game, and because we thus make the acquaintance of a greater number of players on the other side. However, I do not want to argue that point, and I know that a great many people, having a reasonable and natural desire to hit their own ball for half the day, think otherwise. My contention is that the more bloodthirsty and energetic part of the day's work—the singles—should be done in the morning, the friendlier and more easy-going in the afternoon.

There are those who hold that if the singles come first then the foursomes should count two points apiece. I remember to have played in matches wherein this system was adopted. It does away with the danger of one side actually winning the match by lunch-time, but it has never proved popular, and, much as I love foursomes, I am not going to defend it with vehemence. It does seem to give a disproportionate value to one form of the game at the expense of the other. I may be unduly influenced by my recent grilling and gruelling in the sunshine, but at present I am disposed to risk the match being virtually over at half-time and get the hard work done first. Powder first and jam afterwards is the order of events we learned in our childhood.

There is, of course, one ideal method of playing golf on a summer's day, if only the players have time enough, and that is by one morning and one evening round and a long and blissful snooze between lunch and tea. How often have we felt and said, as we start home weary after the day's golf, "Now would be the time to start." There is nothing so heavenly as an evening round when the heat of the day has abated and part of the course is in shadow. Yet we only play that round, as a rule, when it is the only one possible after a day's work in an office. On a holiday we have not always enough self-control to wait for that divine coolness. We pound away in the sun, and when the right time comes we are prostrate. There was a time—ah! well a day!—when a single in the morning, a foursome after lunch, and a four-ball match in the evening, appeared the ideal distribution of a golfing day, and we lashed out more joyously in the four-ball match than in any other. I have my old diary to prove that I really did play that four-ball—yes, and sometimes after two singles. In the abstract I am still of my old opinion, but in the concrete I hold that the four-ball must be abandoned and the foursome be the evening round. Now and again I play an evening round with a young friend who dashes down from the City. We do not get to the course till about seven, and we finish at nine, or sometimes, if there are fat, slow, and obstructive persons in the way, rather later. The valley in which lie the last five holes is in complete shadow so that we feel suddenly almost cold; the greens are becoming dewy so that we have to remember to hit our putts harder at the end than we did at the beginning. We carry few clubs and carry them ourselves, and when we have finished we go home, warm, unkempt, but happy, to a cold supper. The meal is as delicious as the round, and, as the great John Nyren remarked, "the smell of that ale comes upon me as freshly as the new May flowers."

THE LADIES

Every afternoon, as I sat down to try to write an account of the mixed foursomes at Worplesdon, I meant not merely to describe the day's play but also to indulge in some reflections of a general character.

They would doubtless have been both profound and original had I ever had time to think of them or space to write them down; but there were always so many facts clamouring to be related, so many sparkling three's and calamitous eight's, so much "allonging and marshonging" to the nineteenth hole, just when one had settled down in a peaceful corner. The reporter had so much to tell that the philosopher never had a chance. I have had time now and, even so, the generalities are not nearly so numerous or so exciting as I had hoped. In fact, there is only one thing that I really want to say. It can be summed up in the words of Mr. Turveydrop, "Woman, lovely woman, what a sex you are!"

He said those words, we are told, "with a very disagreeable gallantry" and I trust that my reasons are free from that objection. I think I like watching women better than men because their golf is more interesting, and it is more interesting because of their wooden-club play; this is more accurate than that of the men, and there is more of it. It may be that nothing can give quite so exquisite a thrill as the difficult iron shot perfectly executed, but day in and day out, that which excites the wildest hopes and the deadliest fears beforehand, the greatest relief and enthusiasm when it has been well played, is the brassy shot. And how well these modern ladies do play their brassies! Time was—I speak now as an unchivalrous adversary—when one might hope for a fluff or a top unless the lie were perfect. To-day, were I playing, the best I should hope for would be a shot so good that it found a bunker believed to be out of reach.

And then there were the wooden-club shots played at the short holes. These, too, were admirable in their accuracy and often put the man and his iron to shame. One of the great gathering places at Worplesdon is the terrace in front of the club-house overlooking the fourth green. It is there that all but the insanely conscientious await the players, getting a hazy view of the happenings at the first three lowland holes and avoiding a climb. If ever at this fourth hole one saw a ball behind a tree or in the heather there was a lady with a brave smile and a mashie-niblick about to play it. If there was a ball on the green there was a complacent man with a putter. There have always been two schools of thought at Worplesdon as to the holes at which the men should drive, and once it was an argument in favour of their driving at the evens that the fourth and the sixteenth were too long for the ladies; it was inhuman to demand such shots from a poor, weak woman. To-day the ladies bang the ball up on to those greens with their spoons as if it was the easiest thing in the world, and they keep on banging them straight.

Admittedly—and this is a reflection to console the senile—a certain spurious reputation for straightness can be gained by extreme shortness. Many a ball that reposes blamelessly a few yards from the edge of the rough would have gone into it had it been harder hit; but this argument really will not do as regards the modern lady's driving, for she hits the ball very truly and accurately and she is far from short. Now and again she is cruelly out-driven by the opposing man, but, generally speaking, she keeps within hail of him and sometimes she gets in front of him. "Do you generally outdrive Mr. So-and-So like this?" a young lady was asked jocosely in regard to a famous adversary. "I don't know" was the answer. "I've never played with him before."

I have made my compliments to the ladies with the utmost sincerity. At the same time I spy an opening for a little mild propaganda. I wish that the long-driving young gentlemen could and would see that golf would be for them a far better game, more amusing, and more testing, if they had to play it as the ladies do and play brassy shots up to the flag instead of heaving up ball and divot with a number something. Golf as played to-day by the best ladies is golf at its best; the holes are of the right length for them, and they have to play them as Providence or the architects intended; they cannot destroy the proper geography of a hole. To my mind it was more interesting and more exhilarating to watch the ladies at Worplesdon than to see the professionals crushing the fine two-shot holes at Muirfield (what a bitter mockery to call them so!) with their Juggernaut strides.

It is very easy to talk and very difficult to do anything. A course that should make the best modern men play brassy shots to the green would leave the ladies with little to hope for but dull five's, while some of us would never get up at all. We read that for the next Open Championship Hoylake is to be over 7,000 yards long; such stretching of the course may be necessary, but it is not in the least cheering to hear of; it opens up no real way out of the difficulty. Perhaps there is no way, but, if there is, it lies in doing something to the ball and not to the course. Meanwhile let us be thankful to the ladies for giving us a glimpse of what golf ought to be.

AUTUMN COMES

The time of autumn golf has come, and it would be the pleasantest of the whole year if we could forget that winter golf was hard on its heels. The touch of wet on the grass, the freshness of the air, if they did not tell us that summer was over, would promise delicious rounds. It is the only defect of these October days that we have to snatch them; we must gather our mushrooms while we may.

Yet, considered from another aspect autumn is, perhaps, the most cheerful season of the year. The golfer has come back from his holiday, and it is then that he dreams the wildest dreams. The holiday itself is seldom a season for hope, because there is not time for hoping. It is true that the golfer on his holiday tries this and that, and often believes that he has got it at last, but disenchantment follows so quickly and so regularly on attainment that it loses much of its bitterness. He has scarcely had time to pin his faith to his elbow, before he has discovered the emptiness of all elbows and turned to his foot. Life is a long series of little disappointments, rather than a single great and tragic one.

When a man comes back to work on the other hand he has time for reflection; he has been wandering in a crowded mist of styles; now the mist clears and he sees exactly what he was doing wrong all the while. He can even remember the round in the middle of the holiday when he was on the very verge of the great discovery, only to be led away in another direction by some perverse will-o'-the-wisp. Yes, that was undoubtedly it, there was a feeling about that particular shot. It was stupid of him not to recognise a thing so obvious at the time, but better late than never. Therefore, the days that elapse between the return home and the first Saturday round are filled with hope, and, given a week, with no chance of sobering disillusion, hope can grow insanely high.

Again the golfer finds it at first pleasant enough to get back to his own course and meet his own partners and opponents. Their characteristic waggles had possibly grown a little tiresome after eleven solid months, but now after an interval he is glad to see them again and to play the old familiar holes. That is an entirely sane and rational pleasure, but here also insanity lurks waiting for its prey. As a rule, the home course is something shorter and easier than the seaside one where the holiday was spent; it is not afflicted by those winds which are, as Mr. Guppy would say, "enough to badger a man blue." Consequently for the first round or two, golf may seem a comparatively simple game; the gentle suburban breeze does not sweep the ball a hundred yards off the line; if that ball is blown into trouble it can be got out again and is not battered in vain against the remorseless walls of Strath or the Hill bunker. The poor fool actually comes to believe that he has improved and that his holiday resembled a visit to one of those spas which undeniably make a man feel like a limp rag at the time, but are alleged to make him feel like a young Greek god when he gets home again.

This autumnal hopefulness is, in reality, only that which buoys up many golfers from Sunday night to Saturday morning all through the year, but, owing to its slightly exaggerated form, it may endure throughout October with no more than the ordinary ups and downs. With November comes a crash; the golfer finds that he is getting shorter and shorter. If he would accept the fact, which is patent in the case of his friends, that the ground accounts for it, he might be tolerably happy; but the experience of many Novembers has not convinced him, and he goes out practising in the secret dusk in search of that vanished length. There is a particular part of a particular London course that is haunted for me by the friendly ghost of an old gentleman, who was puzzled by this autumnal mystery every year till he was over eighty, and never solved it at last. Let us hope that on Elysian courses there is neither deceitful run nor disillusioning mud.

With regard to this painful subject of mud, I met the other day the sternest and most conscientious of all parents. His home is in a county of clay, so that except on his yearly visit to the greatest of seaside courses he scarcely hits a ball. Not only that but he will not allow his small boys to do so, lest their swings should be corrupted by delving in the mud. I can testify that they swing like dashing young angels, and I look forward to tottering round on a shooting-stick to watch them in future championships; I wonder if a little mud would really hurt them. I recall such good fun in such squelchy fields in my own boyhood that I feel a little sorry for them. I wish they might be allowed just once, on Christmas afternoon, let us say, when they are full of plum pudding. If they solemnly promised to play winter rules and tee the ball they surely could not come to much harm. There is something worse than muddy golf, and that is no golf at all.

HOME AGAIN

It was sad to go away, but there was one sadder than we were. Ever since the hold-all had made its first prophetic appearance in the passage, Johnny, the black spaniel, had been in an agony of apprehension lest he should be left behind. On the fatal morning he had been with difficulty dislodged from a car that was not his, and few more miserable objects have ever sat hunched in a railway carriage. A banging door, which sounded like a gun or a spitting fire, brought him to a full stop in the corridor, thereby holding up for some seconds a procession of luncheon seekers, and when he reached the dining-car it was only with a languidly polite interest that he accepted cheese. Even the end of the train journey brought no balm, for he hates cars worse than trains, and had to be huddled and fenced in among bags of clubs. It was only when the car hooted at the familiar corner and turned through the familiar gate that at last he cheered up. A moment later he was a free dog, his paw upon his native heath, investigating well-known landmarks with an air almost frisky, and obviously declaring that there were no smells like home.

Our own emotions were rather more complex: yet, on the whole, we were not sorry to be back again. It is possible to have enough of a good thing, even golf, and we had had an almost solid and entirely heavenly month of it. The wind is whistling as I write. There is a certain satisfaction in reflecting that it will not bowl me over on to my nose all the way out nor besmirch my record, which in fact I kept proudly to the end, of not having been a single time in Strath during a whole month. The lowering clouds bring with them no hesitations as to mackintosh trousers; there are no doubts and fears as to drawing a number, only the certainty of having to catch the nine something train.

Of course, we feel that we ought to have made more of the first few days that went so deliciously slowly before the turn had been reached and the dreadful rushing away of the second half began. Yet, has not a holiday been a triumphant success when we can say at the end of it, that the journey there was not the best part of it? Another cheering thought, is that if we did not play so well as we had insanely hoped, neither did we play half so ill as we dismally expected. We had our "moments of glad grace" and were not so utterly stale that we could not enjoy the last round of all.

Every golfer has his own private and personal reflections at the end of a holiday, and I give two of my own merely as samples. I never remember before to have had so long a spell of golf without ever experimenting with a fresh putter or even a fresh style—to give it a courtesy title—of putting. On the other hand, I never remember to have tried so many new styles of driving (of course, they all looked exactly the same), which one after the other flattered to deceive. Old Tom Morris was once shown a new putter which its proud owner had just bought, and after duly feeling it observed, "Aye, you'll be very well pleased with that for a day or two." So it was with my styles of driving. I cannot remember one which gave any pleasure after two days. What a lesson, and how often I have pointed it out before, and how often have I failed to profit by it!

I suppose no one has ever come back from a holiday without realising the profound truth of the statement, that history repeats itself. We look back and see that there were a few holes that we generally played well and a good many more that we always played badly. I gave one happy example of my own as to avoiding Strath (and the Hill bunker too) and I could give many more unhappy ones. Day after day, I made a fiercer resolution on the sixth tee to drive on the Aerodrome, telling myself with ever greater emphasis that there was a whole parish to drive into on the left. Day after day I, in fact, drove too much to the right, teasing that double row of bunkers that lie greedily in wait among the heather. Day after day, in answer to the unspoken appeal in my eyes, my caddie said, "I'm not sure, Sir," but I was always sure, and I was almost always right; I was in one of those bunkers yet again, and the bunkers at St. Andrews really are bunkers; there is nothing to do but get out and be thankful.

More instances, equally distressing, come flooding back, but I will give no more. The gentleman who first said that history repeated itself was a highly sagacious person, but that other gentleman who said that familiarity bred contempt was, as regards golf, an ass and an idiot. On the contrary, it breeds an intolerable and unconquerable respect. Time can do marvels, and it may be that on some other holiday I shall always drive like an arrow to the Heathery Hole; but that is afar off and I cannot at present imagine such a thing. Besides, if that time ever comes there will be a hideous compensation; I shall spend my life in Strath, wailing and gnashing my teeth.

There is a friend of mine who has a phrase culled I think from some philosophical writer, which he applies pathetically to his own golf; it is, he says, "ever not quite." Well, no golfing holiday is ever quite, but this was as quite a one as I ever hope to have and I can only hope that there are many golfers, now returning to work, who have as grateful hearts and as good reason for having them.

THE LOST LEGION

The other day an advertisement caught my eye—only a coy, shrinking little paragraph, yet so seductive in its modesty that it has been all I could do to restrain myself. It came from a Railway Lost Property Depot and announced that there were "forty sets of modern golf clubs" to be sold at a guinea or twenty-five shillings the set and that they were "all guaranteed."

It is that last phrase, with its fascinating touch of mystery, which has nearly broken down my resistance. What exactly is a guaranteed club? Is it guaranteed to make me hit the ball? The words bring back dim memories of Shirley's Leading Cases and the "debt, default, or miscarriage of another." Will the railway company answer for the default or miscarriage of my strokes if I buy their clubs? They are the most confiding people in the world if they mean that; yet they seem to have said so in writing. There was once advertised for sale a putter which "made every stroke practically a certainty." That was a bold declaration, but then there was that mean little word "practically" to save the vendor's face. I am almost afraid that "guaranteed" is merely in the nature of a puff or flourish. The irrepressible Pinkerton in "The Wrecker" called his Thirteen Star Brandy "Warranted Entire" and was proud of the words as being "real, copper-bottomed English." When it was pointed out to him that they were usually applied to the public-house and not to its beverages he remained wholly unabashed and remarked, "It's effective anyway; and I tell you, sir, it has boomed that spirit." I suspect these deep dogs of railwaymen of an equally cynical frame of mind.

At the same time, let me do them justice. They do not desire to sell me those clubs like so many pigs in pokes. On the contrary, with transparent candour they assure me that I can "view" them. That makes me think them deeper than ever since everybody knows that the man who views a club in a depot, or anywhere save on the green grass of the links, is lost. Who is there that has not bought a club in some great emporium under the impression that it was the very image of his old favourite and borne it home in triumph and brown paper, only to find that the two clubs are exactly dissimilar in every possible respect? Is it the oilcloth on the floor that does it or the pink paper round the handles? I know not, but that there is a subtle and malignant spell at work is sure, and that magicians' den, the depot, would cast it over me yet again.

There are sometimes to be seen exposed outside a pawn-broker's or a general dealer's shop bundles of old clubs at highly attractive prices. They, too, are bewitching and I can only make myself pass them with a quickened step and an averted eye. It is not that they are superficially alluring, for their shafts look old and bent, rust lies thick on the iron heads, and they are not "guaranteed"; but in the very heart of the bundle might be found the one club in the world which is like the pot of gold at the rainbow's end.

At first sight my advertisement produces a wild beating of the heart, an insane hope. A re-reading of it brings a less selfish feeling, a sober sadness. Think of all the poor fellow-creatures who lost those clubs! It is hard to imagine how they could do it, but since careless people leave diamond necklaces in cabs we must assume that they may leave a driver in a railway carriage rack. It is possible that even a whole bag full of clubs has been deposited in a cloak-room and never recovered. "When will you be wanting them, sir?" the polite porter has doubtless asked. "Oh, about six to-night," the owner has replied, as he hurries off to the City. And then something has happened and he has never come back. Has he caught a fleeting glimpse of a fair face at a window which has changed his whole life? Has he emptied the till under sudden and overwhelming temptation? Has he had a fit or has he merely and incredibly forgotten? At any rate, the bag of clubs has first been put away from its handy place on the floor to some remote shelf, and thence, in course of time, it has gone to the depot, unclaimed and, as we must suppose, unwept, to herd with outcast umbrellas and walking-sticks.

To any golfer who has ever lost a favourite club these tragedies must appear almost too poignant. I am not sure that I should like to own a set of lost clubs; its owner might haunt me with nameless, reproachful eyes, so that I could not keep my own eye on the ball. To buy a lost dog must give, at first, as I imagine, something of the same sensation. We should feel that his real allegiance was not due to us; that he wagged a dutiful rather than a loving tail. We should not know what his lost master had called him and must affront him by a new name. So it must be with irons bought at the depot. Though they are described as "modern" I take leave to doubt whether they would be a numbered set. We should have to re-christen them, and suppose we were to call by some such vulgar name as "jigger" that which the vanished owner had called his "little approaching cleek." He may have heartlessly abandoned it, but he may not; he may have taken all proper precautions:

> "'Tis but a box of modest deal;
> Directed to no matter where;
> Yet down my cheek the teardrops steal—
> Yes, I am blubbering like a seal;
> For on it is this mute appeal:
> *With Care.*"

Despite that inscription the club may have gone astray and the owner be mourning it now and for ever. The thought is too horrid. I will not go a-hunting in the depot.

WRITING ABOUT GAMES

"I hear you write," said a kind clergyman the other day. "That must be very nice." It was a remark to which it was difficult on the spur of the moment to make exactly the right answer, as indeed had been his previous one as to whose Archdeaconry I lived in. Thinking it over afterwards, I was grateful to him for phrasing his observation in such general terms. Had he ever heard of me before—and there was no earthly reason why he ever should—he might have said, "I hear you write about golf." That would not have been quite so nice.

If one is ever known, however slightly and in however small a world, for doing one thing it is not easy to do any other. I imagine that the artist who paints sheep or birch trees by a pool or cavaliers riding out of a castle gate is regarded with some suspicion by the dealers if he ever paints anything else, and may get his picture left on his hands into the bargain. So it is with a "sports writer," to give the poor wretch the most loathsome possible label. It is thought that the cobbler ought to stick to his last, if indeed it is ever discovered that he has tried momentarily to desert it. He ought not to complain, however, for it is a good thing to have a last, a single subject about which he is supposed, often erroneously, to know something, and so to be capable of producing an article, if necessary at short notice. Although I now like to write about other things, at least as well as about golf, and am trying to do so in this very book, yet if I had not had golf as a standby and a starting-off place, it is fairly certain that I should not have written anything at all, but have pottered on unhappily at the Bar. So, whatever I do, I must not be ungrateful to golf, which has been fun and bread and butter for so many years.

Besides, it is, as the clergyman said, very nice. I like writing about golf or about any other game or sport, if I know ever so little about it. If you are excited yourself, there are few things more exciting to write about, and it is a subject, like any other, on which it is possible to write well or vilely ill. This may seem an obvious truth, but I think many worthy people doubt it, regarding all writers on games as sunk in a common degradation. Why they should, it is difficult to understand, unless they have never read Hazlitt's Fight or Cavanagh the Fives-player; or Borrow on Ned Paynter, and Tom Oliver; or Tom Hughes's School House Match at Rugby; or Mr. R. H. Lyttelton on Cobden's over; or John Nyren at Broad-halfpenny; or the Druid's account of Tom Smith, "the mightiest hunter that ever rode across Belvoir's sweet vale with a horn at his saddle-bow." And those are but a few. To carry the catalogue into the realms of the living Mr. Neville Cardus's account of Lancashire at Old Trafford can make the blood dance in the veins. Mr. George Lyttelton on Eton v. Harrow in *The Times* is annually a perfect joy. There is to be found as good writing on sport or games, as simple and clear, as spirited and racy and moving as on almost any other subject; as good models to follow, however faint and pursuing. They will certainly not be followed, however, by somebody who only cares for games and does not care at all for writing. The notion of writing about games, as an idyllic life in the open air, is one which often appeals to young gentlemen just down from the University and without any particular job. When they have consulted me, I have been pleased and touched by their doing so, but I have often been, I am afraid, rather discouraging, not because they will probably earn little money, but because they seem to think that the writing part of it is so easy as to be a purely secondary consideration. Some eminent newspaper personage once remarked that a good reporter was the noblest work of God. That referred, I think, to the power of seeing rather than writing. As far as games are concerned, it is certainly most important to see and to understand what you see. For that reason I always want to read, if I can, somebody who has himself been out there in the middle amid all the agony and tension; who knows what it feels like and does not heap abuse on some poor wretch's head because he "had only to hit a brassy shot to the green

to win the match" and strangely failed to do so. I remembered
Mr. R. H. Lyttelton, whom I mentioned before, saying of
Cobden's over that merely to be able to bowl a straight ball
at such a moment was no small thing. Neither is it such a
small thing as it might seem fully to appreciate that fact. It is
very important, but it is not enough, and those who are
conscious of it in every fibre of their being, when watching the
struggle, are yet sometimes incapable of "getting it across."

Those who write about games have greatly changed their
methods in the last thirty or forty years. I am talking, of
course, not of the great ones whom I have cited, but of us of the
rank and file. Once upon a time no one ever suggested that a
player missed a catch or a putt for the palpable reason that he
was nervous and overcome by the importance of the occasion.
Putts when I first remember them in the newspapers—and, of
course, they get much more space now than they did then—
were always missed "carelessly" or "unaccountably," and
that though the reporter could almost see, if he had eyes and
if he were looking, the club trembling in the delinquent's
hands. To-day we have by comparison "gone all psychological," perhaps too much so. It is possible to write to excess
about "the appalling strain" and so on. Yet it is a fault on
the right side, in that it does convey to the reader at peace in
his arm-chair that the player has had something to endure.
We also deal much more familiarly with the players, very
often too familiarly, I think; but I have said that elsewhere in
a golfing chapter. Generally speaking, we have let ourselves
go more. That I venture to say is a good thing, if we do not
let so much of our excitement get into our ink as to make it
frothy; nor spatter such epithets as "heroic" too freely about,
and in saying that I may very well be throwing stones when
living in a glass house. I remember on one occasion discussing
a writer on games with Mr. E. V. Lucas, most fastidious of
authors with a touching passion for cricket. I praised him and
E. V. would not have it, declaring that he "overwrote" and
that it was just as easy to do that as to underwrite. Of course,
E. V. was right in principle and he was right too in so far as
that this particular writer did sometimes become a little too
lyrical and was much better when he held himself in; but he
had the real fire in him, and that was the important thing. I

once had a pretty little compliment paid me in an after-dinner speech by that admirable professional golfer, Charles Whitcombe. He said that I did not present him and his brethren with bouquets when they won, but gave them nice little buttonholes. I only wish I deserved it. At any rate, I have never forgotten, and have tried to live up to it since. To see a man hitting a ball skilfully and resolutely is to experience a number of pleasing emotions, but if we let ourselves go too unrestrainedly about him, there are no words left for the man who wins the Victoria Cross.

Similarly, it may be worth pointing out that to miss a stroke is not a crime, nor he who misses it necessarily a black-hearted scoundrel. "Try to remember," wrote Horace Hutchinson in his first little book, *Hints on Golf*, "that a person may be a most indifferent golfer, and yet be a good Christian gentleman, and in some respects worthy of your esteem." That is sound advice, sometimes difficult to follow as regards an erring partner in a foursome or the people in front that keep us back, but surely not excessive as to some poor devil we are only watching, who is doing his best. It is not fair to the critic to ask him whether he could do any better himself. Possibly he would not be a critic at all if he could. Yet, this aspect of the question must not be wholly overlooked, and in games I think those are nearly always most lenient who have themselves played in decent company and on at least some moderately important occasion. It is so easy to talk, so hard to do.

I like, as I say, to read someone on games who has been there himself. So, I think, does anybody who knows anything about the subject. Yet in some ways, as regards the purely picturesque, I am not quite sure that it is not a disadvantage to know too much. He who has played with the men whom he is describing or with their predecessors ought to be able to appraise them justly, and will not be led away into facile admiration of something that is little more than a happy chance. He ought to be able, discarding the immaterial, to see the point on which the battle really turned, and his only grave danger ought to be that of being too technical. He sees the player in rather a different light from that of the ordinary spectator. He sees him as an eminently fallible human being and not as a demi-god. He ought to write better on that

account, and he probably does, but he may not go so straight
to the heart of the great ignorant enthusiastic public. I keenly
enjoy watching Rugby football, but I have never played it,
and so there is much that I miss altogether. "Foot up" is a
mystery, and I cannot appreciate to the full the play of the
forwards. Only the obvious is really beautiful to me, a perfect
passing run of the three-quarters that finally sends the wing
man in by the corner flag. So in reading an account of
the match I find the gentleman, however wise and however
illustrious, who tells me at length about "packing, 3, 2, 3"
rather a bore. I prefer him who piles on the superlatives, even
if he does it inartistically, and shouts aloud about Wooller
"crashing through with his giant stride." That is because I am
ignorant and, though I may suspect that the writer is not in
a much better case, yet I sometimes enjoy his fireworks more
than I do the sober, well-informed person who has told a
plain tale well. The flamboyant impostor would nauseate me
about golf; but alas! I sometimes suffer him about football. I
suppose this is not only ignorance on my part; it is bad taste
as well, but these two things often go together.

That is why in more cynical moments I wonder if it is a
pity to know something about one's subject and flatter myself
that being untrammelled by knowledge I could write a good,
honest, exciting account of Wooller myself. Certainly, if I
tried it would be a mass of the purplest patches, but, then, I
saw *the* match, the rubber match between Wales and New
Zealand at Cardiff when Wales won. The mere going there
on the Friday night was worth the money, with people singing
and talking Welsh in the corridors and no single thought in
the whole train but of the match. It was Hazlitt's account of
going to the Fight come to life. Next day there was the drive
into Cardiff with the whole road crowded with men from
the mining valleys, a dozen of them at least, as one of my
companions said, "in Dai Jones's taxi"; the fear of fog and
the breaking through of the sun at the last moment; the almost
unbearable emotion of "Land of our Fathers". As to the
match itself—but I must not do it. Enough that there was
Wooller, sure enough "with his giant stride"; Claud Davey
almost burying himself in the sacred soil as he scored the first
Welsh try right between the posts; the luckless Tarr being

carried off; Wales getting the lead again with fourteen men and hanging on to it; the man in front of me who sat with his head in his hands, murmuring, "Why doesn't that bloody whistle go?" Then came a punt to touch by Idwal Rees that made all safe, so that my companion said, "That's like laying a putt stone dead when you're dormy." Finally, there was the strange hush of the Welsh crowd as we came out into the street. None of the "Here's tae us! Wha's like us?" but the silence of prayer answered. I could have written three florid columns about that and there would been no word of packing 3, 2, 3. I did not write them, however, and with a few no doubt lamentable exceptions have stuck to the game that I know something about. A little while before I began to write golf for *The Times* I believe that nearly all the games in the paper were written by one man, who was called Sporting Ward to distinguish him from Humphrey Ward. A very kind, friendly creature he was, and I believe he knew a reasonable amount about a reasonable number of games, but the days of such omniscience are past.

As I said before, some people think that writing about games is an idyllic life. For that matter, there are a good many who hold the same view about any kind of writing. "Nice, easy life they have of it, too," said the young lady in Kipps's emporium. "Write just an hour or so, and done for the day. Almost like gentlefolks." It would certainly be ungrateful in me to deny that my kind of existence has been a pleasant one, though it has, like any other, its dreary and exhausting moments. To report an Open Championship, for example, in wet weather is not all bliss. Play goes on all day, and if you watch with a reasonable conscientiousness, write two accounts of what you have seen, or heard about, and throw in a broadcast or two, you will find by dinner-time on the third or fourth day that you are rather tired. Nor is the task made easier by the fact that you are surrounded in the club-house by temporarily happy and idle persons, who are watching only for fun, and do not always fully appreciate the fact that you yourself have got a good deal to do in a hurry. They periodically ask such questions as, "Do you send your stuff by post?" How they imagine that it gets into a paper printed that night, I have never been able to determine.

However, these prostrating days do not come very often, and I may add that I used to play as well as write, and that once I succeeded in reaching the semi-final of a championship and writing one account for London and one for America each day. Moreover, I felt extremely well and strong at the end of it all. As long as you are winning and so feel cheerful at the end of the day the writing comes trippingly enough. The collar-work begins when you have been beaten and think you ought not to have been. In one of his last Championships Horace Hutchinson, who was then playing very well, though he grew easily tired, sent home a telegram each evening: "Still alive." Then one sad day came the message: "Stone dead." Horace did not, in fact, write daily reports of championships, but I have quoted the words of the telegram because they so succinctly express the feeling of ultimate defeat. Stone dead you do feel for a little while, and you are strangely disinclined to sit down and write. Nevertheless, as Mr. Pope remarked, "some strange comfort" attends every state, and perhaps it is a good thing to have to write instead of thinking gloomily about the putts you missed in the intervals of listening to the stories of the putts that other people missed. To-day, when I play no more, I sometimes say wonderingly to myself:

"Pray, how did you manage to do it?"

for I find the walking and the writing quite hard enough work.

I have, of course, taken the examples best suited to my purpose. On the other side must be set many easy-going days of comparative loafing in the sunshine, or watching something that does not matter *too* much from a stationary point of vantage in agreeable company. That is wholly enjoyable, and if I spoke just now with a moment's peevishness of the people in the club-house, I did not really mean it, for it is the friendliness and the companionship that makes the life so enjoyable. A good day, a good match on a good course, a good friend with whom to watch it, and I ask no better. Moreover, when you have been on the road as long as I have you have friends to meet you wherever you go. I sometimes feel quite ashamed of the number of nights all told that I have stayed under endlessly kind and hospitable roofs on these occasions. There is scarcely a place in England, Scotland,

Ireland or Wales where Championships are played where there is not also one of these delightful houses, and I hereby lump them all together and write them this joint and several "Collins". If they do not know by this time that I am grateful, then I must be inarticulate indeed.

The blessing of friendliness extends far beyond the boundaries of golf, for to have played one game is something of a bond with all game-players, and the pleasure is the greater if you are, as I unashamedly am, a hero-worshipper. One of the greatest festivals of the year for me is the University Sports. In one sad respect it can never be the same again, for dear Parson Tindall used to come to lunch with me and then take me into the rarified and glorious atmosphere of the "Blues Stand." There I have met heroes—yes, I will use the word—whose names my pen falters in inscribing: F. J. K. Cross, of whom I first read in my dear "Badminton" on athletics; C. B. Fry, whom I saw do the long-jump record when I was a schoolboy; Fitzherbert and Barclay, great Cambridge quarter-milers; Rudd, Milligan (who talks to me kindly about Scottish murders); the list is endless. It was there, too, that I first saw Mr. Macaulay and heard him say something that has stuck in my mind ever since. Rudd and Butler had just dead-heated in the Quarter; the whole world was temporarily mad; the two runners themselves lay on their backs on the turf, panting and shaking hands. "Well," said somebody. "What did you think of that?" "A nice quarter," answered Mr. Macaulay gently. "A nice quarter."

So to be taken into the pavilion at Lord's is to encounter all manner of agreeable and eminent people, and there is, too, a very particular luncheon at the University match, strongly Harrovian in tendency, with me the lone Etonian, at which I meet annually Mr. A. J. Webbe and Mr. M. C. Kemp. Best of all, perhaps, is the annual golf match at Rye between the club and the Harlequins, headed—or they used to be headed —by Ernest Smith and Johnnie Evans, with the illustrious H. D. G. Leveson Gower to provide the definitely lighter side of the entertainment. I love cricketers, and feel that I can at least talk something of their language. Oarsmen, I admit, frighten me just a little, but they are very friendly, and do look quite beautiful when they come out in all their ancient finery at

Henley. Rugby internationals can be a little frightening, too
—after dinner; but what of that? As Mr. Snevellici remarked
of the ladies: "I love 'em, I love 'em every one."

I love the game-players, and yet for me the pleasantest thing
in writing about golf has been to be read now and then by
those who are not golfers. I have, alas! a very small "fan
mail." When I read some gentleman who says that his remark
last week about something or somebody has brought him "a
flood of letters," I cannot help—no doubt it is a loathsome
trait in my character—wondering whether a modest trickle
of letters has not swollen a little in his imagination. At any
rate, no postman has ever groaned under mine, but such
letters as I do get nearly always begin with the statement that
the writer does not play golf, or that twenty years ago he
bought three second-hand clubs and has long since broken
them, never to be replaced. If after that he says civil things, I
swell with vanity, for it shows that I have been true to my
principle of spreading the golf thin. To write for ever solid
golf is soul-destroying, but to have it as an excuse for writing
about things in general is good fun, even if at the end one is
a writer only amongst golfers, and a golfer only as compared
with the writers. It is, I am afraid, especially good fun if it
enables me to quote from Dickens and Thackeray or *The
Wrong Box* or the *New Arabian Nights* or Calverley or
Sherlock Holmes. It is no doubt a maddening habit, and yet
I believe it is a real bond with readers who are also fond of
these works. Indeed, I think it would be possible to make out
a very sufficient apology for quoters. They do not indulge
their propensity, as is generally thought, in a desire to show
off. They do it partly because they come to think in the
language of their favourite books, and partly because the mere
writing down of some heavenly phrase gives them a rich
physical satisfaction not to be resisted. Occasionally they are
in a Pickwickian sense humbugs. That delightful person and
writer Mr. A. B. Walkley regularly quoted "wery fierce" and
"'eres richness", but in fact his acquaintance with Dickens
was extremely superficial, nor did he ever pretend otherwise.
Generally, however, it is all that the quoter can do to restrain
himself from quoting a great deal more than he does, so strong
is his passion. I admit that he makes one feel rather small

sometimes if one does not know what he is quoting. Hazlitt, who I take to be almost the arch-quoter, defeats me continuously, and yet I like him the more for it, and besides he had great excuses, for he died seven years before *Pickwick* was written.

To writing about golf has of late years been added broadcasting about it, and I suppose that one is heard by far more people than have ever read a word one has written. I am not conscious of it at the time, being rather convinced that when the announcer speaks my name all the listeners in the world simultaneously rush to their wireless and turn it off with all the savage satisfaction that this simple act can give. Yet there must be some who do in fact listen, such as the old lady—I think she must have been old—who wrote me once a furious letter. Not once, but twice, in some account of a championship I had in the excitement of the moment used the word "devil"; somebody had, I think, holed the devil of a long putt. She would not soil her pen with it, expressing it only by a blank, but conscience told me what she meant. Never, she said, had such a word been used in her presence before, and would I another time please remember that there were ladies and young children listening to me. I only hope she did not hear my friend Captain Lyle describing the finish of the Derby that very same summer, and saying that it was the h—of a race. She convinced me that the humblest person gains in broadcasting a new public, however small. My real attainment of a momentary fame came, however, when I gained my spelling international cap against the United States. On the following day both the man who cut my hair and the waiter who brought me my lunch at a club congratulated me with an almost fierce joy on having helped to defeat the Americans. That was, by the way, an experience both amusing and alarming, and I never propose to risk again the escutcheon which I bore untarnished from that stricken field. It was in the early days of the revival of spelling bees and the words were, to be sure, extremely easy; but some allowance must be made for the importance of the occasion and the garish lights all around. There was, too, the fact that every time one's turn came round one had to advance to the microphone through a network of coils on the floor, carrying one's own coil to which the headphones were attached, like a lady delicately picking up her skirts on a muddy day. Both before the contest, when we had tea, and afterwards over a triumphant cocktail, I observed both in myself and some other members of the team a tendency (like that of Mr. Dent Pitman) to "giggle like a venturesome schoolgirl at a picnic." The B.B.C. had chosen their team for the occasion with care and, as I suggest, with a shrewd and practical eye to victory. Each one of us was supposed to represent some particular walk of life and I, as I blush to record, was supposed to be an athlete. My opposite number on the American side was a real athlete, a long-distance runner of distinction who, so we were told, was by profession a seller of newspapers, in the street. I cannot help thinking, I hope inoffensively, that I had an initial advantage over him in spelling. He was a gallant trier, and his rendering of "faun" as "phawn" ought without demur to have won a point. That was not all, however, for our "business man" had got a first in Greats, which somehow seemed a little out of character, and even our Colonel was a Colonel in the Education Corps. As to our schoolboy, he was the most confident and immaculate speller I ever met in my life. Our literary gent was Sir John Squire, our announcer Mr. Howard Marshall, and altogether we had a strong all-round team. The Colonel stumbled accidentally and rather ironically over "Camaraderie" (so did the American Colonel, who began "Com"); but otherwise we were faultless, except for our two ladies. One of them did let the side down a little, and both found "Rhododendron" too much for them, which may or may not be an argument for a classical education. We had plenty in hand when that mishap occurred. Some minutes before time had expired we knew that we were more than dormy, and had revenged the previous defeat of an Oxford side with too many blues in it, who would never have been spelling blues.

That, however, is not golf, and broadcasting about golf has been up till quite lately a leisurely amusement, of which the recorders of other games must feel envious, since it consists only of giving an eye-witness account not of what is happening, but what has happened. For all I know, those peaceful days may have gone for ever. The Americans have, I believe, regularly running commentaries on their championships given by speakers perched high on moving towers, and the same thing was tried here, rather tentatively, in the summer of 1939. I had always greatly admired Captain Wakelam keeping up with the pace of a Rugby match, or Mr. Marshall finding something entertaining to say about every ball of a featureless maiden over. Only on attempting to do likewise did I appreciate their true greatness. This was at Birkdale during the English Amateur Championship. Once, talking out of the side of my mouth into an odious little pocket microphone, I tried to follow and describe the playing of a hole from behind. Birkdale is a place of giant sandhills and with my lame leg I felt very like John Silver ploughing his way through the sand in the great scene at the block house. Later I was teed up immobile on the top of a mountain and described, shot for shot and filling up the intervals as best I could, the play at the fourth hole, which turned out entirely commonplace, with every stroke perfectly dull and respectable. The first attempt was said to have been inaudible, whereas the second was audible, but whether this was really an advantage must be doubted. It is possibly prejudice on my part, but I am convinced that golf does not lend itself to this form of description. Television is a different matter, for then seeing is the main point and the broadcaster but an accompanist. He need not fill up with padding all the intervals of inaction; indeed, he must be quiet with all the rest in the world while the putting is going on. I took part in the first televising of a big match —Bobby Locke and R. A. Whitcombe at Coombe Hill—and it would have been very enjoyable but for having to do the talking not in privacy, but surrounded by spectators, who took a hideous interest in the performance. They were as heartless as passers-by who look over the shoulder of a poor wretch painting a landscape. I could have wished, too, that the hills of Coombe Hill had not been quite so steep when it happened that I had to be in two places at once. Still, when it was finished it seemed "all wery capital," and I felt much as I had done years before when I had had a brief in a County Court and it was all safely over.

Once I broadcast a duologue on golf, if that be the right term, with Harry Graham. The precise subject has escaped me, but I know we went on too long, which was not exactly our fault, and I doubt if it was a success. But it would have been if I had dared or we had been allowed to carry out the brilliant and audacious scheme which he proposed. This was that we should pretend never to have met before, and be introduced to one another at the microphone; that we should for a while get on better and better; that I should in turn call him Captain Graham, Graham and Harry, while he became familiar with me by corresponding stages; that we were then to have a violent disagreement, rapidly decline in friendliness and end by addressing one another as "Sir." It was a notion amongst notions, but I knew my own utter lack of histrionic ability, to say nothing of a tendency to giggle; so it remained only a great conception. That he could have carried out his part of the scheme to admiration no one can doubt, and I cannot refrain from saying here what a really heavenly person he was, with the softest of hearts and, when in the mood, the most racy and entrancing of company. The fascination was enhanced by the fact of his looking so extraordinarily unlike what he really was. He was genuinely witty, full of original and amusing ideas and a most conscientious artist in the neatest of verse. Yet at first sight he appeared not the typical Guardsman, if indeed there be such a thing, but the kind of Guardsman of the lady novelist, the kind that is too good to be true. There was a little story of his which tells far more quickly what I am labouring to say. He was one day in a famous bootmaker's shop, being tried on, "with one boot off and one boot on," as he said, when there suddenly rushed into the shop a little lady. Looking at him fiercely, she exclaimed, "Don't you twirl your moustache at me, sir," and rushed out again. The little old lady was presumably mad, but many who were sane might have fallen at first sight into her mistake. He was one of the people one always hoped to meet. The choice between the Garrick and the Beefsteak for lunch involved wondering which he was likely to choose on that day, and either much joy over the right guess or a sigh of regret over the wrong one. And my only real excuse for bringing him into this chapter must be that he wrote the most delightful of golfing poems, beginning:

"I was playing golf one day
When the Germans landed."

Like General Wolfe with Gray's "Elegy," I would rather
have written that poem than—well, than almost anything.